PART I – THE EMPEROR

The Aftermath - July 1815

It was over - the taste of defeat was bitter, foul, sickening - unacceptable! Days later it enraged and depressed him. The return from Russia was intensely awful, leaving a deep scar, but this was worse. This was the end.

He had been on the verge of turning it all around, winning through.

After Elba the margin between success and failure was so small.

The highly improbable seemed possible, victory within reach. The greatest reversal of fortune in history. The consequences monumental.

How the Hell did it happen?

His men had come back to him and fought like lions.

That farmhouse? It was an insubstantial obstacle, thinly defended. It should have broken. They should have broken it!

His plans were sound. He could not be everywhere.

That was no consolation now. There was none to be had, he knew. Just outcomes. He was above all a realist.

Defeat. Losses. Intolerable!

He had raced back to Paris, to control the news and, he hoped, the aftermath. Soon it became apparent this was not possible. He was a fugitive once again. His supporters peeling away, fair weather friends and the faint hearted in the vanguard, bystanders waiting, even loyalists whom he needed if he were to re-group or survive. The Allies were searching for him. He heard the rumours that Blucher and his Prussians were determined to exact final retribution. He felt it.

It all moved too quickly, sand running out. Not fear, just a precipitous downward slide. A horrible sick, hollow feeling. God I am so, so tired.

Having found no advantage in Paris, no lifelines offered, no suggestions accepted, the Allies closing in, meeting no substantial resistance, he had given in to the pleadings of his thinned entourage and made his way toward the Atlantic Coast and, as he now contemplated, exit.

He had been confronted with an ultimatum – abdicate or be deposed. It was over.

A return to relatively comfortable, familiar Elba would not be offered. The provisional Government was pressing him to leave France without delay or face the consequences. He had only a short time in which to try to determine his destiny. On his own terms? But where could he go? Hope for a life as a free man? Certainly not in Europe. They would search everywhere, he would be recognised, and he could not, would not, skulk and hide.

The obvious solution was America. A new country, with whose emerging political ideology he felt sympathy. Its appeal was growing on him.

If, as was agonizingly apparent, France had lost the will to fight, the men and arms, faith in his capacity to win. If he could not garner enough support in the Paris Legislature to pull together and lead again armies of France against the Allies, sufficient to chase them out, to rebuild, then why not go to America? Live as a private citizen, in a land which only recently shared a common enemy? He had doubled the size of that new country by selling Louisiana! Joseph had useful connections.

Perhaps they might have need of his administrative skills? He might establish and lead a new state. Not perhaps the New World empire that he once envisaged, but nevertheless something worthwhile, a working retirement during which he could establish a settled legacy of ideas. A more hopeful thought than much else.

At Malmaison Marie Walewska (*Valevska*), his pretty Polish former mistress, visited with their son[i]. He looked so much like his half-brother, the King of Rome. He so missed the boy!

She offered, begged him, to let them join him in exile, for her boy to be with his father. Attractive though it would be to have female companionship, and sweet and devoted though she was, he tired of her long ago, and the presence of a mistress and their child, manifestly his, would not serve his cause.

What of Louise their little son? Was it possible her father could be persuaded to allow them to join him in America? Could they be brought to him?

A few leagues away, in the disciplined, drilled environment of a Royal Navy ship-of-the-line, HMS Bellerophon, its commander, Captain Frederick Maitland mused alone in his cabin.

The rich, active, varied experience he gained as boy and man in the Royal Navy when Britannia truly ruled the seas had prepared him for just about anything. His capacity for surprise limited.

He had returned to England in October, after a year in command of Goliath (a cut-down 74) on the Halifax and West India stations. At the end of her usefulness, she was paid off at Chatham. In quick succession he was appointed to command the Boyne, fitting out at Portsmouth as the flagship of the Commander-in-Chief on the American Coast, Sir Alexander Cochrane. Having sailed her to Cork, where in January a fleet of transports and merchant ships congregated, they were bound for America.

News of Boney's escape from Elba reached them. Fresh orders translated him to the venerable Bellerophon, famous veteran of the First of June, the Nile and Trafalgar. On 24 May they departed Plymouth with the squadron of Sir Henry Hotham, Maitland issued with sealed instructions.

Events moved quickly. After investigating L'Ile Dieu, Bellerophon arrived off Rochefort, where they observed French war ships anchored. They were joined by Cephalus, an 18-gun brig-sloop, swift and manoeuvrable, with a shallow draught, suited to close blockading river mouth ports.

Soon after the momentous news of a decisive victory at Waterloo – the fate of Europe resolved and Boney on the run - thoughts of years more of war with France could again be discarded – he received a message from an agent in Bordeaux. Boney was likely to try to escape by sea, probably to America, quite possibly via Rochefort. The Atlantic Coast was the most obvious direction of flight and his own patrol zone fitted the case squarely.

The threat represented by two French frigates and lesser vessels at Rochefort had taken on a different dimension. England and France were no longer at war, but if they were under the direction of Bonaparte, they could not on any account be allowed to slip away, even if they had to be engaged and stopped. Once on the open sea it would be a race with bleak odds.

Confirmation that Boney and his entourage were in the vicinity made it immediate. He must prevent escape or face the inevitable music.

On 10 July the schooner La Mouche approached under a flag of truce. Maitland politely and formally ushered Comte Emmanuel de Las Cases and General Savary, Duke of Rovigo to his cabin. They handed over a letter from Count Bertrand. It requested that their master be allowed safe passage to exile in the United States. Maitland told them his orders were to prevent this.

Unable to obtain further instructions in the time available, on his own initiative Maitland offered passage to Britain. Discussions continued over the following days, La Mouche toing and froing bearing Las Cases, General Francois Lallemand and General Gourgaud.

Although he was being informed by Napoleon's ambassadors that he was at Rochefort, Maitland had discovered that Boney was at L'Ile d'Aix. Rochefort was rife with rumours of escape plans. One of the more amusing was that he would be smuggled out in a special cask consigned aboard a neutral Danish merchantman. A cartoonist's delight.

Maitland gave instructions for guard boats to keep a watchful eye around the clock on the Frigates Meduse and Saale (both looked ready for sea), to report comings and goings and, most especially, warn of preparations for sail. The British war ships must be ready to intercept, to fight.

Napoleon's reverie was broken by a gentle knock. Beckoned, five men walked in and stood respectfully, the newcomer clearly freshly arrived. The others (Charles Tristan de Montholon, Henri Gatien Gourgaud, Charles Lallemand and Anne-Jean-Marie Savary), used to being in his company, still in their uniforms, were prominent members of his entourage. de Montholon introduced their companion, a tall strongly built stranger, about forty years of age, well-made travelling clothes, a self-confident man used to an outdoor life. "Sire, this is Captain Henry Graham of the American merchant vessel "Pride of Charleston". He was found by our good friends. He has informed us that he is in Rochefort to take on fresh provisions and other supplies and embarkation of passengers and cargoes bound for America. He might be willing to help us."

Napoleon Bonaparte, self-made Emperor of France, man of history, remained seated for half a minute or so as he examined the face of this seafarer who looked him in the eye and returned the compliment, he was pleased to see. He had long ago acquired the ability to assess the qualities of men - of all ranks and walks of life. After a short interval, not long enough to be rude, he stood and, with the beginnings of a smile, offered his hand, respectfully and firmly received by the stranger. "We are pleased to meet you Captain, be seated and tell us of your ship". Turning to General Lallemand he gestured to pour wine. Napoleon had the capacity of putting others at their ease, gaining them with his charm, humour when necessary, his personal touch. He was likely to have need of Captain Graham.

Graham knew he was in the presence of a man whose fame, or infamy, transcended all others alive. Himself accustomed to judging men, his ship and the lives of those on board depending upon it, he warmed to his host. He had not known what to expect when brought here. An egomaniac, a monster, disappointment? Fascinating possibilities.

He was approached that morning near the dockside by a nondescript older man dressed like any other merchant, enquiring about his ship, his next passage, its whereabouts, speed, cargo and capacity and his willingness to take on important well-paying passengers, discreetly. It had to be interesting, and it was not unusual to be approached by careful voyagers, in these years of turmoil. He allowed himself to be brought to this place with only little explanation. An important man wanted to meet him and could pay him well. It was common rumour that the fallen Emperor and other senior Bonapartists were nearby, seeking escape from their pursuers, blockaded by the British. A great quarry, valuable bounties, all seeking refuge, offering rich payment.

He now found himself in the presence of a smiling man, compelling respect, an intelligent force. "Sir, I am honoured to meet you. I was told we can do business together."

When he left the Ile d'Aix under cover of darkness, to return to his ship, a large deposit in gold coin reassuringly tucked away in an inner pocket, Graham had much on his mind, arrangements to make, partners to placate, his ship's freedom and safety to protect. He had agreed to provide swift direct passage to Boston for Europe's most wanted fugitive and his companions, a fair-sized party of men, wives and children, who would be crowded aboard.

He would remain at Rochefort for up to 5 days, awaiting an opportunity to board his precious human cargo, with as much discretion as could be arranged (a night-time embarkation off the Ile de Lie by boat in smaller groups, luggage also - the details of which he and his new passengers had thrashed out, each finally satisfied with the others' thoroughness). After five days he must leave with or without them. They all understood, by then matters would be decided. In any event no merchant ship could stay still for long. Time was money.

No easy task to remove and board a large party, unaccustomed to the sea, with baggage. Under the vigilant eyes of the patrolling Royal Navy, whose 74-gun two decker ship of the line, and two consorts were off the approaches, ominously and aggressively blockading the entrances to the harbour. Intercepting shipping, keeping a watchful eye on the French frigates, a brig and a corvette lying at harbour.

Since news of Boney's arrival in the vicinity reached the British, Bellerophon had been reinforced with two smaller, swifter 20-gun ships, HMS Myrmidon and HMS Slaney.

Onshore were plenty of spies, turncoats, royalists or proto-royalists and others who would be quick to take advantage of an opportunity for swift and substantial reward. The presence of an American vessel and rumours that Napoleon would try to escape to America drawing close attention on the Pride and the comings and goings of those aboard her.

The thought of running the gauntlet to beat the blockade did not daunt Graham. It stirred his blood. There was nothing new in this contest. Until three years ago the United States and Britain were at war, the Royal Navy pursuing American ships at sea, boarding, press ganging sailors (deemed renegades, owing allegiance to their King) and seizing cargoes and vessels as prizes.

Clippers like the Pride were built for speed, able to outpace all but the fastest British Man o' War. If he could get them aboard and pass Bellerophon and its escorts, once out to sea he was confident he could deliver his passengers to his home port with little danger of intervention. He would enjoy the chase.

He was being offered enough in gold and diamonds to satisfy even his partners. The adventure in it stirred him.

Time passed lost in thought. He and his companion barely spoke. It was evening, dark save for the lights of the townsfolk and still open hostelries, when they got back to the outskirts of Rochefort, where he stepped down from the two seater buggy driven by his taciturn chaperone, the so-called 'friend', "M. Bochet", his transport from the quiet spot on the river where they landed the small boat that ferried them at dusk to and from L'Ile d'Aix.

He walked a circuitous route to his ship. He concluded he was not followed.

In his cabin Graham secured the deposit, washed his face and hands, changed his shirt. After catching up with the ship's news, he sat alone in reverie, barely noticing the simple cold supper brought to him, the wine he washed it down with, or the familiar muffled sounds of a moored ship.

He slept soundly, as only a man who has much to organise and who enjoys events, and their profits can do at the end of such a day. Content.

After Graham left, the four generals remained with the Emperor (for such they would still call him). They were joined by Emmanuel de Las Cases, who had assumed the role of the Emperor's Secretary. Savary recharged their glasses and they waited expectantly for their leader to speak, to reveal the direction of his thinking.

Minutes passed. They were used to this.

"So, Gentlemen, America. Our friends in Paris [was there a trace of irony?] have put at our disposal the Meduse and the Saale, frigates, a corvette and a brig to take us to America, as we asked. The Americans have been friendly. Have reason to be grateful. They have no love for the British. The Royal Navy, destined ever to flout us, has blocked our passage. The new masters of France will not permit a fight. These ships are nearly useless to us, but not entirely. We can create a diversion, while the good Captain spirits us away."

"We have asked for passports for ourself and for you and your families. We are still waiting. As we heard, Graham can take us provided we have these passports and permission from the United States Minister, William Crawford to land in America. Again, the request has been made. We cannot voyage to America and present ourselves as fugitives seeking sanctuary."

Las Cases was the first, "Sire, and how will we proceed if the passports are not given or the Americans say no, or more likely, do not reply in good time? Surely Paris will not risk angering Louis or the Allies, nor will Crawford risk the peace with Britain. They will not help."

Napoleon looked at him, "nevertheless we will ask". Las Cases replied "Sire, you must consider surrendering your person to the British before you are captured. There is very little time. If you are captured anything can happen."

After a minute's heavy silence, Napoleon nodded, saying "thank you, Gentlemen, it is time for dinner".

When they were all congregated with the ladies the atmosphere was jolly, feverish, almost surreal. The jokes funnier than usual, the laughter louder, nervous. The Emperor was at his most gracious and warm. Danger was galloping towards them and their future was opaque. They could all feel it. For themselves and this man in their midst to whom they owed so much and to whose destiny they felt bound, by individual degrees. Uneasy companions.

The Emperor enjoyed the meal and then read to the party, holding court, as was his custom, in good times and bad, until even he was ready to say good night. They were grateful to be together, to enjoy this taste of normality and companionship. This was the best time of the day. No more serious matters were discussed.

Later when they had withdrawn to their sleeping quarters in lowered voices and whispers husbands and wives discussed their situation after their own fashion.

13 July 1815

The day started well enough. The mood among was superficially gay at times, though fragile. Madame de Montholon suggested a morning walk, with which the Emperor and so her husband and Las Cases readily agreed. Others followed some paces behind the main group, led by the Emperor who had graciously offered Mme La Comtesse de Montholon his arm. The others, attuned, had noticed her effect of lightening his mood and were grateful for it.

After an hour, during which the Emperor inspected the fortifications of Fort Liédot and teased and probed gently those of the pretty Mme de Montholon, they returned to find a worried looking visitor pacing, in dusty travelling clothes, anxious to speak with the Emperor, with whom he withdrew behind a closed door. The others making themselves apparently busy within reach, waiting for news. The arrival did not augur well.

Ten minutes or so later the door opened, their visitor emerged, stony-faced, nodded to those present and took his leave. Bertrand, Gourgaud, de Montholon, Savary and Las Cases were summoned by the voice from within. Once more the door was closed.

The Emperor stood before the window at the far end of the room, looking to the sea, his hands behind his back. He turned; his visage ominous.

"The news from Mr Crawford is that we will not be welcome in America. Crawford says he cannot grant us entry to the United States without the approval of President Madison and there is of course no time to obtain that. We are "too hot to handle" it seems. The Americans do not wish to antagonize the British, or indeed anyone else now that they are at peace. This is the gratitude we receive for our support, for doubling the size of their country!" He paused, adding "and we have lost the Saale and Meduse on the orders of Louis".

The significance of these statements hung in the air. The full realization that they were helpless rats in a swiftly closing, probably lethal trap impressing itself on each of them.

Las Cases, "Sire, your only option is to surrender your person voluntarily, to give your parole to the British, to the Commander of the nearest Royal Navy ship. The British are the most likely to treat you as men of honour. Asylum in Britain is the only realistic choice. Time is running out. You must not fall into the hands of Louis, the Austrians or the Prussians. I beg you to act, or anything may happen."

de Montholon protested "We have discussed this before. The British Government hates you. They will parade you as a trophy of Waterloo." The debate raged. Bertrand, finally, agreed with Las Cases.

The Emperor, who listened but not taken part in these exchanges, said quietly "I cannot abide the idea of living among my enemies."

A sparrow flew in through the open window. Once it settled and ceased its fluttering, Gourgaud caught it swiftly, gently in his hands, "a portent of good fortune, your Majesty", he said, stroking its head with a forefinger and proffering it. The Emperor looked at the small bird empathetically and pointed toward the window – "there is enough unhappiness about, at least we can free this little one - release it". They all watched, as the bird seemingly determined their fates.

After it set off in the direction of the open sea, and British ships, Napoleon turned and said "Las Cases, you and Savary will approach the British Captain today to make the arrangements. Bertrand you will write a letter to the Captain and also a private letter from us to the Prince Regent, which Gourgaud will deliver, as Las Cases and Savary will arrange. The letter must be delivered into the hand of the Prince Regent by you personally. We will entrust ourselves to his care and generosity. Perhaps they will treat us with the same hospitality offered to Lucien.[ii] Now that Louis has returned there is a vacancy in England. Gentlemen, we have much to do." The matter was decided.

An Emperor of France, even one who has abdicated, cannot be seen to wilfully adopt the life of a fugitive.

Napoleon wrote to the Prince Regent:

*"Your royal highness, confronted with the various factions that divide my country, and with the enmity of the greatest nations of Europe, my political career has come to an end, and here I come, like **Themistocles**, to sit at the hearth of the British people. I put myself under the protection of its laws, which I request to your royal highness, the most powerful, the most constant, and the most generous of my enemies. Ile d'Aix, 13 July 1815. Napoleon"[iii]*

Not far distant, Maitland was in a state of nervous excitement. He did not have time or means to consult higher authority if he was to secure his quarry before his other, foreign, pursuers. His orders (as given to his fellow blockading captains along the Atlantic Coast) were to prevent the escape of Bonaparte. He knew that by taking him on board, accepting his parole and taking him to England he was interpreting those orders liberally. Surely that was initiative? Better than refusing and turning him away to a more uncertain fate, more difficult reports and explanations?

Maitland agreed to dispatch HMS Slaney, a 20-gun sloop, under Captain George Sartorius, with General Gourgaud aboard to Plymouth urgently and thence to London to the Prince Regent to deliver Bonaparte's letter, a firm pre-condition of his surrender. Sartorius would bear a letter from Maitland to the Admiralty. Gourgaud left France on 13 July.

During that last day on Ile d'Aix the Emperor met with his advisers, preparing for what was ahead. He spent a long time closeted alone with Karl Schulmeister, who departed as quietly as he came. A notorious man whose effectiveness depended upon operating unobserved in the shadows.

As best he could, the Emperor arranged his affairs, prepared and despatched letters and messages for his family, his supporters, his agents, his bankers and others. He was a renowned master of planning and logistics, with an exacting eye for detail. He enjoyed this familiar activity. Planning and preparation were key, he knew of old.

It was a frantic day of comings and goings, packing and preparation. Time was running out and all felt the imminence of their pursuers. The British had come to represent a welcome source of refuge. A foe more predictable and less vengeful than the chase inexorably drawing in.

It was uncertain that they would see France again, or when, they were acutely aware, most particularly the man who had brought them to this moment.

A message was delivered to Captain Graham. His valuable cargo would not be coming aboard. The Pride should sail. He might be called upon again and should keep the deposit against the day.

15 July 1815

In the early morning Napoleon boarded the French brig Epervier, which made its way slowly toward Bellerophon. The wind conditions proving unfavourable,

Maitland sent the Bellerophon's barge to intercept and transfer the Emperor.

At 7am, the great man, wearing his famous green Chasseur's coat, preceded by General Bertrand, was received respectfully and with ceremony - including a 21-gun royal salute - aboard HMS Bellerophon, to the obvious excitement and curiosity of its officers and crew and all ashore who had seen him depart. Ever mindful of the moment, the erstwhile Emperor of France, this meteor, the man who had become a force that crashed into, terrorized, modernized and ruled over much of Europe and excited and enthralled the remainder, raised his hat, bowed and said in French to the Bellerophon's proud captain, "Sir, I am come on board and I claim the protection of your Prince and of your laws".

Maitland greeted his guest with formal courtesy and ushered him below to his own cabin, vacated for the purpose. At Napoleon's request Maitland introduced the ship's officers, following which the great man, mindful of the evident respect and courtesy shown to him, of his effect on others, and demonstrating his capacity to engage with fellow military men, said "Gentlemen, you have the honour of belonging to the bravest and most fortunate nation in the World." He made a very good first impression.

Matters did not proceed as hoped. Life on board the Bellerophon was agreeable enough, but his thoughts of a comfortable retirement in the English countryside were soon curtailed. News of his capture and intended landing, along with General Gourgaud, reached London before the Bellerophon arrived.

Napoleon had placed great trust in Gourgaud. A man who had fought bravely in many battles, among the first to rally to his cause after Elba and who twice saved his life. In Moscow where he found and put out the fuse lit by Russians to explode some 500,000 pounds of gunpowder and at Brienne where he intercepted a Cossack's lance. After Waterloo Napoleon appointed him, already his "Premier Officer de Ordnance", Brigadier General and his Aide de Camp.

Charged with delivering his master's letter into the hands of the Prince Regent, Gourgaud failed. The British would not allow access to His Royal Highness. He returned to the Bellerophon with the letter.

Napoleon would have been very disturbed if he had known what was developing. de Montholon was wrong. Maitland had misjudged.

His Britannic Majesty's Government wished for no living trophy. The Cabinet was concerned over the uncertain consequences of bringing into the country the most famous man in Europe, their greatest enemy, feared, loathed and admired, an object of widely held curiosity.

There was radicalism and unrest about after many years of costly wars with France and in America. Anything could happen, as the 100 days following Bonaparte's escape from Elba had demonstrated. It had been a "close run thing", they were acutely aware. But for the arrival and intervention of Blucher and his Prussians and untimely delay in French reinforcements arriving on the field of battle, Europe would be facing a different future and Bonaparte would be dictating terms.

The Prime Minister, Lord Liverpool, who had steered the Britannic Ship of State to victory, wrote to Lord Castlereagh, Foreign Secretary, in Vienna discussing the future of the Continent in conference with the representatives of the other great powers: "We are all very decidedly of the opinion that it would not answer to confine him in this country.... He would become the object of curiosity immediately, and possibly of compassion in the course of a few months, and the circumstances of his being here, or indeed anywhere in Europe, would contribute to keep up a certain degree of ferment in France...St Helena is the place in the world best calculated for the confinement of such a person...the situation is particularly healthy. There is only one place...where ships can anchor, and we have the power of excluding neutral ships altogether... At such a place and such a distance, all intrigue would be impossible; and, being so far from the European world, he would soon be forgotten."

Aboard Bellerophon, while these matters were debated onshore, Napoleon demonstrated his remarkable capacity to win over the affection of even his recent enemies. He inspected the ship, showing considerable interest in her running. Each day he walked the deck at about 5pm, followed by dinner taken promptly at 6pm. His habits were regular. He was, for such a senior prisoner, amiable with both officers and ordinary ratings, showing interest in their activities.

In turn the ship's company warmed to their guests and sought to host and entertain them as best they could aboard a ship of war. On 18 July, two plays, The Poor Gentleman by George Colman the Younger (first published in 1802) and Raising the Wind by James Kenney (1803), were performed by junior officers of the ship's company.

Plymouth

They arrived off Plymouth on 26 July, dropping anchor in Plymouth Sound. Soon they learned that they were to be isolated, incommunicado, even the crew were to remain on board and no private letters were allowed to be sent ashore from anyone aboard the ship, crew member or passenger.

For days they were marooned awaiting instructions from London. News of his arrival having preceded him, there gathered large crowds of sightseers paying to gaze through telescopes from the shore. Many hired rowing boats to take them out for a closer look. Napoleon obliged good humouredly, promenading on deck, taking the air, raising his hat to those ladies who caught his eye. He hoped to win over public opinion and it helped to relieve the boredom. So many were in competition to come up close that Maitland deployed boats and crews to keep the overly inquisitive at a distance. During these uncomfortable and anxious days for the party aboard such a welcome boded well, raising their fragile hopes.

On 31 July, in the mid-morning, Napoleon graciously received Major General Sir Henry Bunbury, who introduced himself as His Britannic Majesty's Under Secretary of State for War and the Colonies, and Admiral Lord Keith, Commander-in- Chief in the Channel, an old, no-nonsense Scotsman. Both were received with naval formality and then with all the decorum and ceremony that the Emperor's entourage could muster. It was far more than either of the envoys was comfortable with. Boney was a defeated prisoner, their long-standing enemy, a tyrant and in no position to bargain or cavil, let alone hold court!

They were serious men come about a serious matter in determined mood. The sight of hundreds, maybe more, sightseers and apparent well-wishers in the harbour and around the vessel day-tripping in a carnival atmosphere served only to irritate them.

Being greeted on deck by Bertrand, Gourgaud and de Montholon in the uniforms of French generals was perhaps to be expected, and their entitlement, but their deferential references to "the Emperor" and "His Majesty" were too much. Brusquely they declared that they had arrived to speak with "General Bonaparte". By the time they were ushered into the great cabin to meet this unique curiosity, for even they were intrigued and undeniably, grudgingly excited to meet him, they were confirmed in the justification for their nation's sentence.

The cabin was crowded, airless on this warm July day. As their host motioned them to do (which also irritated – damn it, this was a Royal Navy ship-of the-line and he

24

their defeated prisoner!), Sir Henry and Lord Keith sat at the dining table facing Napoleon. Bertrand, Las Cases, de Montholon, Savary, Lallemand and Gourgaud did not take available seats but stood behind their master.

Brandy and wine were offered to the guests and accepted (Napoleon took wine; he avoided spirits).

Pleasantries observed, including a toast to The King and The Prince Regent offered by Napoleon, Sir Henry got to the point. The French contingent composed, inwardly apprehensive, charged, awaiting sentence. Newspaper reports suggesting St Helena as their probable destination of distant exile had reached them; they still hoped these were incorrect or that, by some miracle of persuasion, their leader could change this unsettling fate. It was a tiny spot at the other end of the Earth. It might as well have been the Moon.

Sir Henry spoke, "General, I am instructed by His Majesty's Government to deliver to you its decision concerning your future situation and maintenance and the restrictions to which you will be subject."

There was a pause, silence, gulls squawked outside. The now familiar creaking, muffled thumps and shouts of the daily business of a Man-o-War at anchor in peacetime.

He was as a judge pronouncing sentence, cognizant of his moment in history, speaking for his nation.

"You are to be transported to the Island of St Helena, in the Indian Ocean. There you will be housed and will receive an allowance and provision for a small household which will allow you to live out your life in adequate comfort, safely out of harm's way. You may take with you such members of your party as His Majesty's Government may approve and servants of your choosing, limited to three officers and twelve domestics. Generals Savary and Lallemand may not go with you."

The sentence hung in the air for what seemed longer but was in reality minutes.

All eyes were on Napoleon, whose facial composure visibly turned to stern cold anger. We can only speculate at the racing thoughts of Savary and Lallemand – the British (the Bourbons?) patently had something different in mind for them; retribution.[iv]

Napoleon glared at Bunbury and Keith and said tersely, "my blood should rather stain the planks of the Bellerophon than will I go to St Helena. This mean and infamous decision will throw a veil of darkness over the future history of England. After three months in that place I will be dead." With that he stood up rapidly and paced to the large window at the stern of the great cabin, his back to those present, his hands held behind him. The audience or meeting, depending upon perspective, was ended.

Ceremony at an end, pleasantries over. Bunbury and Keith made their exit.

On their return journey to London, lost in thought, they spoke little of the meeting, other than to observe in irritation on Gallic pomposity. They felt a sense of anticlimax. They had been dismissed summarily, but their task was accomplished. What else were they to expect?

Napoleon turned to face his lieutenants. "Well, so it is true", he said. "They fear me even now. They fear their own people more" (he gestured toward the boats and the shore). "They want to punish me but dare not go further. I am to rot and die a 'natural' death in poor conditions at the other end of the Earth or be forgotten, or both, they hope". He paused, "and they may succeed".

Amid protestations of anger, defiance and vehemently anti-English sentiments by de Montholon and Gourgaud (who had re-joined their company, reporting on his reception and interviews in London), Las Cases spoke "Sire, you must send a message direct to the Prince Regent, appealing to his sense of justice. Only he can change this decision. We have only enemies among the English Cabinet."

There was little or no hope, but another letter was written and sent, also without response.

The Emperor spoke in private with each of Savary and Lallemand before they departed. As for the remainder of his party, he told them that they were not obliged to join him in his distant exile. He would understand if any of them decided to remain. To a man they protested their willingness to accompany him.

Napoleon later spoke with Maitland, telling him "It is worse than Tamerlaine's iron cage. I would prefer being delivered up to the Bourbons. Among other insults…they style me General: they may as well call me Archbishop!" He then informed Maitland, who did not object, that he would be convening his party, including the servants, to break the news.

Crowded into his cabin (Maitland's erstwhile cabin), Madame de Montholon and Fanny Bertrand (who was English and could choose to remain) seated, the senior members of the remaining party behind him, facing the others, some pressed against the panelled wooden walls, they listened to their Emperor. There were reactions, from resignation, anger and belligerence ("let's fight and set fire to the ship, then they will have to take us ashore") to barely hidden distress. The Emperor called for quiet and they filed out.

Later that evening Fanny Bertrand tried to jump over the side, stopped only by de Montholon, who remained nearby, having observed her odd and unhappy behaviour.

There was to be no delay. Liverpool wanted this exotic captive and magnet for popular attention safely departed and far from the shores of England, the Continent even more so, as soon as could be arranged. No time could be allowed to give opportunity for deviation or intervention from any quarter. The next day those who were to travel to St Helena and their baggage were transferred by small boats and re-embarked aboard HMS Northumberland, an 88-gun ship-of-the-line, under the command of Rear-Admiral Sir George Cockburn KCB, Bt.

As preparations for the disembarkation of the French party from the Bellerophon were in train, de Montholon approached Captain Maitland with the information that his master wished to make a gift to the Captain of a box containing his portrait set in diamonds, in gratitude for his gentlemanly conduct towards him and his entourage. Though gratified, Maitland felt compelled to decline. Later, upon his departure, Napoleon pressed upon him as a memento a tumbler bearing the crown and cipher of Josephine. Saying goodbye, in the cabin he was now relinquishing, Napoleon said warmly to Maitland "my reception in England has been very different from what I expected, but it gives me much satisfaction to assure you, that I feel your conduct to me throughout has been that of a gentleman and a man of honour".

Maitland wrote "it may appear surprising that a possibility could exist of a British officer being prejudiced in favour of one who has caused so many calamities to his country; but to such an extent did he possess the power of pleasing, that there are few people who could have sat at the same table with him for nearly a month, as I did, without feeling a sensation of pity, allied perhaps to regret, that a man possessed of so many fascinating qualities, and who had held so high a station in life, should be reduced to the situation in which I saw him".

Cockburn was a lifelong naval officer, a highly respected, popular, brave and resourceful 43 year-old veteran of the French Revolutionary Wars, the Battle of Cape St Vincent, the Napoleonic Wars and the American War of Independence. He had directed the capture and burning of Washington a year earlier. As Second-in-Command of the North America Station, he had patrolled Chesapeake Bay and other areas of the North Atlantic coast relentlessly blockading commercial shipping and attacking ports, seeking to strangle the supply routes to the American rebels and to undermine their finances. Lord Liverpool and the Admiralty knew he was just the calibre of man to ensure the safe and uninterrupted delivery of his charges to their far-flung destination and to remain some months to settle them in, as he was instructed to do, as newly appointed Governor of St Helena and Commander-in-Chief of the Cape of Good Hope Station.

Cockburn was altogether a different proposition to the less experienced Maitland.

Cockburn received his guests on board and installed them in their quarters. He observed the arrival and storage below decks of their seemingly vast array of baggage, with polite courtesy and inward amusement. Napoleon would have the great cabin, where they would dine together. Given the extent and nature of the provisions loaded on board and the astonishing arrival of Franceschi Cipriani (*Franchesky Chipriani*), Napoleon's maître d'hotel, his butler and pastry chef Pieron and Lepage, his cook, despite the limited facilities for preparing food aboard a Ship-of-the-Line, it was clear that simple seaman's fare was unlikely to be on the menu and that even the rather better offerings an Admiral might customarily expect on his table would not do. There would be compensations!

There were, naturally, heightened curiosity and varying degrees of excitement among the officers and crew of the Northumberland and a sense of pride. Theirs' would be an historic voyage in peace time when many other crews and officers were being laid off or put on half-pay. They would be crossing the Tropics, rounding the Cape, carrying the most famous passenger in the World. Something they could dine out on, tell tall tales about, relate to their children and grandchildren. No-one was unmoved, impressed or not, implacable foe or just plain curious. The ship was abuzz, all could feel it.

Napoleon's entourage comprised twenty-six people, the maximum he had been allowed. A company of the probable and the seemingly improbable - all tying their uncertain fates to that of their now fallen hero and leader, the man by whom they had been made, elevated and given purpose. Who can know all of the personal motivations, complex or simple? A microcosm of a court combined with the vestiges of an army commander's staff.

Gourgaud, initially not on the list of those chosen to accompany the Emperor, pressed his case for inclusion with Bertrand, resulting in Napoleon interceding and putting him on the list, displacing Nicolas Planat.

Among those to decline the questionable honour of joining his patron in exile was the Emperor's private doctor, Louis-Pierre Maingault.

Aboard the Bellerophon Napoleon had met the ship's surgeon, Barry O'Meara, an Irishman and Protestant, fortuitously, as it turned out. Napoleon had discovered in O'Meara an empathetic, skilled and experienced naval surgeon who unusually spoke Italian, having served in Sicily and Calabria. Napoleon's request that O'Meara should become his personal doctor was agreed to by Cockburn – after all, who better to keep a close eye on their captive and his health?

Napoleon was touched that Paola, his sister, Princess Borghese, offered to forsake Rome to accompany him.

The British refused.

The voyage

At first his good humour and internal composure evaporated after he was informed of his destination, his sentence.

Disabused of the quixotic notion of a comfortable retirement as an émigré gentleman of note in England, he contemplated the 4,400-mile voyage and his destination alternately morosely and furiously.

The ability to recover, to think quickly, strategically, laterally and to adapt and surprise were hallmarks of his life and success. He could think and take action while others froze or reacted. He took stock.

At least he would have familiar and loyal company, plus some physical comforts. He would have picked and capable lieutenants. With such men there would be possibilities. In the meantime, his valets (Marchand and Noverraz), Mamluk Ali (his valet and guard) and others of his loyal household (the brothers Achille, groom, and Joseph Archambault, coachman, the footman Gentilini, the fellow Corsican and usher-barber Santini and Rousseau the lamplighter and toymaker) would maintain his routines and provide for him as he was accustomed. Even so, he thought, he was used to the deprivations of campaigning and the economic ups and downs of life – he had experienced both wealth and great power and paucity of means. He was used to adjustment, used to overcoming new challenges, more than that - it was his trademark.

He was not a natural sailor and rough seas made him queasy. In calmer conditions Napoleon enjoyed the sea air and learning about the workings of this substantial fighting vessel. Sailors were soldiers at sea, as were the complement of Royal Marines aboard and they warmed to each other's presence and curiosity. The atmosphere was friendly. Napoleon had a way with such men, accessible and totally self-assured. This was Boney in the flesh and close by. Who could not be impressed?

Colour was ensured by the inclusion in the party of the attractive and intriguing Albine Montholon, contrasting the wrought, unhappy and apprehensive Fanny Bertrand – making her poor husband's life a misery. They were accompanied by the three Bertrand children and three-year old Tristan Montholon. Children are resilient and more adaptable than adults, given adventure and kindness and soon they were enthralled by their surroundings, the strange workings of the ship, the bustle and the sights of the voyage.

While the presence of women and children aboard a Royal Navy war ship was not welcomed by all of the Northumberland's complement, the majority were happy to experience this rare exposure to domesticity, their own homes and loved ones distant. With children language is no barrier.

The long voyage in the main passed without incident, though most of the French except Gourgaud suffered from mal de mer.

There were a few high points, such as celebrating the crossings of the Tropic of Cancer and the Equator, anchoring in the harbour at Gibraltar to pick up fresh water and victuals and sighting the North Western shores of Africa. These afforded Cipriani, Pieron and Le Page opportunities to create imaginative treats and surprises.

The most irritating event was the confiscation by Cockburn of some 4,000 gold Napoleons, funds needed to smooth their paths - anticipated though this inconvenience had been (to preserve anything they must be prepared to give up sufficient to avert further searches).

Relations between Admiral Cockburn and General Bonaparte, as he called him to his intense irritation, remained cool, civil.

St Helena

After a voyage of ten weeks, on 15 October 1815, HMS Northumberland dropped anchor in James Bay, St Helena's only harbour, set against an impressive backdrop of black cliffs 600 feet high, flanking Jamestown, the only town, of some 100 houses.

The ship's arrival and anticipation of their famous new resident had the islanders and the garrison agog with excitement. A new governor was news enough, but the arrival of the Great Ogre was the most significant thing that had ever happened in their small cut off world in the South Atlantic.

For two days Napoleon and his party remained aboard as accommodation on shore was prepared. In the early evening on 17 October they landed.

The transfer by barge to shore and landing of Boney and his colourful, obviously foreign entourage and their substantial baggage and possessions were watched with great curiosity. This infamous magnetic man walked slowly along a line of spectators standing silently behind soldiers with fixed bayonets (to protect the new arrivals). A Grenadier exclaimed "they told me he was growing old; he has forty good campaigns in his belly yet, damn him!" The Emperor was amused and recounted this pleasing remark to his companions that evening.

There was a carnival atmosphere, though on a smaller scale than in Plymouth. The curiosity was mutual – Napoleon and his companions were equally interested (and frankly concerned) to take in their new, obviously limited, surroundings and to observe its inhabitants, the New World which was to be their cage, his final home if Great Britain and the other European powers were to have their way.

They were informed by Cockburn they would be installed at Longwood House, on the unhappily named Deadwood Plateau, until recently the Lieutenant Governor's residence, now being refurbished and extended to house its new occupants. In the meantime they were to squeeze into the Briars Pavilion, in the grounds of the home of an English family, the Balcombes.

That night Napoleon stayed in a house in Jamestown, his companions spread across other quarters – some, including Las Cases and Gourgaud, housed in a hotel.

The next morning Napoleon was taken on horseback by Cockburn to see Longwood. They called in upon the Briars on their return, where they met the Balcombes. When afterwards Bertrand teased the 32 year-old bachelor Gourgaud that he should marry the vivacious 14 year old Betsy Balcombe – producing a sharp riposte – Napoleon intervened, telling Bertrand not to speak of it again – he would find him a wife in Paris.

The Briars Pavilion, as they soon discovered, provided barely enough accommodation for their sizeable party. They found that William Balcombe, his wife Jane and their four children, were interested, friendly and respectful hosts, very sensitive to the needs of their extraordinary guests.

Only 16 year-old Jane and the younger Betsy spoke French well enough to bridge communications. William Balcombe, a merchant Superintendent of Public Sales for the East India Company that owned the island, soon became a diligent purveyor of the substantial quantities of catering supplies, wines, brandies and other consumables and goods required to meet the demands of the French household. Opportunity finds beneficiaries in the most unlikely places.

Once she overcame awe, fear and shyness, Betsy found their visitors to be different, fascinating, warm and friendly. She soon struck up friendships, most particularly with the Great Ogre himself. They charmed each other, this man of legend and vast worldly experience and the young girl with touching innocence.

She soon came to call him "Boney", which when first spoken brought the reply "but I am not at all bony", looking down at himself bemusedly. This familiarity was allowed to no one else and caused some consternation within the former emperor's contingent, forbidden such impertinent familiarity.

She amused him, as did the effect on those around him. She helped him with his efforts to learn English and to learn about his new surroundings and the occupants of the island. Betsy was a ray of sunlight.

News of their friendship soon reached Europe, where many continued to be fascinated by 'news' of the erstwhile ruler of France. Ungenerously, some speculated that this was a love story.

Almost as soon as they moved into the Briars Napoleon began a campaign of complaining of the conditions on the island. He instructed his companions to do the same.

On 20 November a ball was held at Plantation House by Admiral Cockburn, to which the senior officers, Allied Representatives, Napoleon and the senior members of his entourage were invited. It was the most exciting event in the social calendar, and a welcome distraction. It amused Cockburn to instruct Gourgaud to dance with Betsy Balcombe, but the Frenchman had eyes for another English lady, Laura Wilks. To no avail.

Their time at Briars Pavilion soon passed and on 10 December 1815 they were moved to Longwood, extended and refurbished.

While larger than Briars Pavilion, Longwood House was still not capacious and was afflicted by its miserable location, high in the centre of this generally temperate island, on the pessimistically named Deadwood Plateau. Longwood was shrouded in cloud for more than three hundred days a year, offering winds, damp and high humidity.

The Emperor declared angrily to all the clear intention of his captors to finish him off in this desolate and remote spot on the globe!

They discovered the comprehensive - and expensive - precautions taken by the British authorities to ensure there would be no escape, no rescue, no repeat of the return from Elba and all that had followed. There were many loyal supporters of Bonaparte, his large and still wealthy family, rumours of rescue plots, and while alive it seemed he would always offer a potent threat to the order of things, as he had so recently demonstrated.

Two Royal Navy frigates patrolled the seas surrounding St Helena, constantly on station, capable of seeing off any vessel likely to attempt a rescue or landing. The absence of suitable anchorages other than James Bay reinforced the island's sea defences. A coastal landing was too difficult, dangerous for boats and men, seas and currents strong and treacherous, the island a rocky fortress.

Sited nearby at Deadwood Barracks was a large contingent of regular infantry. A flag station had been installed so that signals could be sent regularly to the Governor, informing him of Bonaparte's situation (such as "All is well with General Bonaparte") or, God forbid, sending an alarm if he escaped ("General Bonaparte is missing"), and other predetermined messages.

All of these measures were made known, or otherwise became apparent, to the Emperor and the experienced soldiers in his party, for whom it was a simple matter to reconnoitre, under the pretext of exercise.

Cockburn was relieved and replaced by a man who was even less to the Emperor's taste. Major-General Sir Hudson Lowe, a 46 year-old career army officer of broad experience, who had seen active service and been commended for gallantry by the Prussian Generals Blucher and Gneisenau.

He had received his instructions from Lord Bathurst, Secretary of State for War and the Colonies, who wrote to the Duke of Wellington "I do not believe we could have found a fitter person of his rank in the army willing to accept a situation of so much confinement, responsibility and exclusion from society."

Hudson Lowe assumed his responsibilities as gaoler with the utmost seriousness and determination.

He received a warm welcome from Cockburn, who was enthusiastic to hand over and depart aboard the vessel that conveyed Lowe, his mission accomplished. Over an agreeable dinner at Plantation House they discussed their Prisoner and his principal companions, their roles and idiosyncrasies. It was clear to Lowe that Cockburn had not warmed to Boney. That night he went to sleep in his new home with mixed thoughts and feelings about the meeting to come the next day.

Together Cockburn and Lowe made their way by carriage from Plantation House to Longwood.

Lowe observed that Cockburn and General Bonaparte regarded and treated each other with a cool detachment from the outset, exchanging no more than polite perfunctory formalities. No warmth in their goodbyes. It was a short meeting. One of only a half dozen or so that Hudson Lowe would have with his prisoner.

The pattern of life at Longwood soon become established. It was a tight space for the entourage, which included families, to live shoulder to shoulder. Little could pass which was not known to all. Unsurprisingly, tensions and rivalries simmered. They were provided for, for now, but what did the future hold for them? At the centre of this small hive ruled the Emperor Bee.

It had become quickly apparent that the French had prodigious and varied needs. The happy merchants and shopkeepers of Jamestown competed to satisfy. The Emperor, to his great irritation, was not permitted to leave the grounds of Longwood, but other members of his household were allowed the relief of visits into Jamestown, where they ceased to be a curiosity. Gaspard Gourgaud continued to live in Jamestown at the hotel.

Jamestown was a regular port of call on the merchant shipping routes between the Cape, India and beyond. As many as fifty vessels at a time anchored in James Bay, replenishing fresh water, vegetables and fruit, bringing business to the shopkeepers, victuallers and suppliers.

It continued to be the habit of the household to meet for dinner and, often, to gather afterwards while the Emperor read to them.

They all craved news from France, from Europe, the outside world - new stimulation, and perhaps even hope. Rare, dated, newspapers were scoured for all that could be gleaned. A small window on events, fashions, gossip…

Like many an energetic man who finds himself underemployed toward the end of a busy life, the Emperor decided it was time to write his memoirs, a long project which helped him pass the time. Something within his control which allowed him freedom of expression – the only true freedom he enjoyed. It became his habit to retire to his study. He dictated to Las Cases, de Montholon or Gourgaud, an extension of their duties, but it helped to pass the time for all involved. Even O'Meara was an occasional willing scribe. For good measure he wrote a biography of Julius Caesar, a perspective he felt uniquely justified in offering. It was comfortable territory, taking up his abundant time, an unfamiliar experience.

He was enjoying relations with Albine de Montholon, their close proximity translated from dalliance and mutual electricity to sharing of needs and appetites, her room opposite his own.

Napoleon was experienced in the bedroom[v]. He regarded his sexual needs in much the same way he thought of food, drink, exercise and entertainment, necessaries for his physical and mental health. A happy distraction bringing to him some joy in this otherwise miserable place. Albine was desirable, experienced, willing and available, enjoying his affection. She was the compliant mistress to a great man, with which comes a place in history and the possibility of more tangible and immediate rewards. This was not the anxious, exhilarating love of young novices or the furtive affair of commonplace cuckoos.

What of Charles de Montholon? Ordinarily he would have been faced with the dilemma of whether to challenge his wife's lover or to take a more mature and liberal view, that of an aristocratic husband whose heir is secured, and to ignore the affair, which in any event, must surely end naturally. He chose the latter approach; the lover in question was unchallengeable, even protected by his captors. What was he to do, however miserable or slighted he might have felt? He could only look ridiculous or experience worse.

The cold reality was that a pattern had been repeated. His own liaison with Albine had begun while she was married to another man, their wedding coming only two months after her divorce. Neither had inconvenient scruples, neither was a hypocrite. These were the morals and accommodations of the times.

When it became clear that pleasant retirement in England or another acceptable place was not going to be afforded to the Emperor, he began to plan and prepare for a new life. Even before he surrendered himself to Captain Maitland careful preparations were devised. Schulmeister received instructions, sealed coded letters were delivered to members of the Emperor's immediate family, to his bankers in Amsterdam and Switzerland and to his most trusted agents – the spider's web that would ensure his wishes would be met.

Even now, after the 100 Days, after Waterloo, after all that he and his family had lost, so much of what he had carved out through conquest and extraordinary ambition and daring, their hidden wealth - much of it in diamonds, sapphires, other precious stones and gold; portable, concealable and exchangeable, usually untraceable commodities - was huge and well hidden from his vengeful enemies. His private treasury was said to have held in excess of 54,000 precious stones! Croesus would have envied him.

Such wealth engendered loyalty, bought aid, influence, services and possibilities not available to other men, especially when wielded by a military genius who only recently bestrode Europe, his agents, their networks and tentacles still active or available in many quarters. The Bonapartes had friends and there were many who did not welcome the new order in France and in the Italian states; though not all wanted his return and the upheavals that would inevitably follow – few families had not been touched by loss. Across Europe a great many husbands, fathers, sons and sweethearts had not come home, or were broken by war. Aid and sympathy were available, a resurgence was not.

Escape from St Helena was a serious challenge to even his resourcefulness. Developing his plans excited him, as new campaigns always had. Giving up was not in his constitution, nor being captive.

He soon sized up his adversary, Sir Hudson Lowe. The British had sent him just the kind of man he wanted in a gaoler, a man he could keep at a distance and whose character would not question his froideur.

It would not be intelligent to attempt escape too soon. The British and their Allies were vigilant.

The opportunity to write his memoirs, distractions shared with Mme de Montholon, was a worthwhile use of time while plans were formed, arrangements put in place. Plans had to be thorough. To be caught attempting escape or afterwards would probably result in ignominious death. He would be hunted with all the resources and vengeful energy his enemies could bring to bear. His accomplices could expect no leniency either, whether he was caught or not.

Within days of landing at St Helena, the Emperor convened regular meetings of his core staff – Henri Bertrand, Charles-Tristan de Montholon, Gaspard Gourgaud and Emmanuel de Las Cases. From the beginning, once it was clear that they would accompany the Emperor to his place of incarceration, they knew that they constituted the escape committee. Sworn to the utmost secrecy, their loyalty beyond question. Each bringing their own capabilities, the stakes as high as could be.

The hope and prospect of securing the Emperor's escape motivated them for a mix of reasons, not least was it should result in their own departure from the island. They were not prisoners, yet. It was not lost on them that there was humour in their situation – like bandits, pirates or common criminals they were planning the escape of the most famous prisoner of all!

At their first planning meeting, in his study at Longwood, the Emperor opened the discussion, "Well, gentlemen, here we are – at the end of the Earth! I have been sent here to rot and die! My enemies dare not kill me themselves, so they send me to be buried in a godforsaken hole in the middle of nowhere, with a miserable climate in the clear expectation it will finish me off in a few years, far away from our homeland!", he said tersely, his face suffused in deep rage and resentment, his eyes far away. After a few moments, "and they might succeed." They waited to see if there would be more, but nothing came for a full minute.

As if he had come to an internal decision, the Emperor's visage cleared. He asked each in turn for their assessment. Three generals, experienced campaigners, and an atlas maker, educated in military matters, with naval experience. Tacticians all, their leader the greatest strategist of modern times.

The first to speak were the generals, who between them methodically listed problems, the list growing, the barriers mounting. No likely force could rescue them, a well-equipped regular military force of some size and a squadron of warships would be required – and their captors might be under orders to finish off their captives rather than lose them.

They were not sailors and had no capacity to seize a ship, certainly one which could escape the harbour and the patrolling Royal Navy, voyaging a huge distance to a safe haven, if one could be found. They were closely watched, with limited freedom of movement, the Emperor not allowed beyond the confines of Longwood. Communication lines were complicated, involved huge distances and carried a high risk of intervention, the British watching closely all arrivals of ships or persons in the only harbour, James Bay, anticipating covert activities. The prospects looked bleak. They were glum.

When it came to Las Cases, who refrained from commenting on military matters, he expressed the shared conclusion of the Emperor's Staff. "Sire, the only way you will escape is through death." There was evident discomfort among his colleagues, but no disagreement.

A reaction was expected, an outburst. None came. The Emperor smiled, looking at each in turn. "My friends, it is the very hopelessness of our situation which will be our greatest weapon. As you have correctly assessed, there can be no rescue and escape is impossible. I am meant to die here. We shall nevertheless escape." With surprised, hopeful interest, they perked up, stiffening their backs, reminded that their leader had thought and done the seemingly impossible before, countless times. If anyone could.

"I see I have your attention. Las Cases is correct, I must die here. Only then will the British and their allies relax their vigilance, return this place to its former obscurity, forget about us. Only then can we find a place to live a new life, somewhere of our choosing. So, we must die."

They began to protest, but the Emperor raised his hand for silence. "No Gentlemen, we shall not actually die, we must be seen to die, to die so thoroughly and convincingly that there can be no room for doubt, for doubt there will be, examinations there will be. The rulers of Europe will want assurances, certainty, verification. We must make sure they get it. Everyone, members of our family, our loyal subjects, followers, friends must believe it. Must have no thought of seeing us again. There can be no return to France. No more campaigns. I must live quietly, discreetly in exile. Those who recognize me living among them must accept, must believe, it is not me but, as the Germans say a doppelganger, obviously not the deceased Emperor of France. If I were not dead, surely I would go far away and hide?"

The Emperor paused, for them to absorb his words. He knew men like few others, able to take their measure and inspire them to his bidding.

It was transformational. Their lives and careers had been forged in the service of this man. They had followed him into exile across the World to this remote and unwelcoming spot, uncertain of what the future would, could hold. In most cases their families were restless, anxious and unhappy, fearful. The uncertain length of their stay depending upon the strength, health and longevity of their leader, or their willingness and determination to abandon him, with all that entailed, an unhappy dilemma for even the most devoted. Already their horizons had closed in to the near intolerable, such interest as their travels and new situation afforded long since enjoyed and replaced by boredom, frustration, fractiousness and personal dislikes, rivalries and petty insults. To a man they were eager to hear more.

The Emperor continued, "so, if I am to be dead, I must present a body for examination, a body dead from natural causes, which their doctors will confirm is me and that I died in circumstances that close the matter. I must be so dead that it is final, irrefutable and I am gone from the stage." Their silence reflected this inconvenient truth.

"Gentlemen, it is the very impossibility which will be the key to our success, to our freedom. Some of you will remember that Schulmeister has within his circle men who have long been useful to us, precisely because they were able to convince others, at least for a time, that they were us. They deceived our enemies about our whereabouts, even protecting our person. We need to infiltrate one of these men here on St Helena, the most resolute, convincing and loyal among them, to impersonate me, in life and eternally in death. A man willing to sacrifice his own identity and die as me. In exchange we will escape by the means they came."

The others took this in, impressed by the dawning possibilities and the magnitude of the obstacles and pitfalls that stood in the way. Could such a man be found, could he be removed from France and infiltrated onto the island, assume the Emperor's identity and continue without discovery? That was the scale and strangeness of the solution that they were being instructed to plan and execute.

The Emperor continued, for he had their concentrated interest and thoughtful silence, minds whirling with activity, assessments. "That is enough for today Gentlemen. Before we break up, these are your responsibilities. Generals Bertrand, Gourgaud and de Montholon will learn the details of the defences of the island, of the strength, practices and routines of the garrison and the naval forces here, so that we are fully familiar with our situation, identifying any weaknesses we may exploit, especially to effect communications and a possible exchange - when that can be organized."

"Las Cases, you will be our head of intelligence. The only way in or out is through Jamestown. You must all study it carefully, the shipping that comes and goes, the operations and routines of the harbour authorities, the businesses on the waterfront, etc. You must look for opportunities to bring agents and messages ashore and to send them away. Thank you" (and with that they each stood, nodded and left, dismissed).

They left with a refreshing sense of purpose, of relevance.

The Escape Committee met regularly, sharing news and information, building the picture of their situation and receiving such information and news as their leader chose to share. They were long since used to this method of operating.

The Emperor had arrived on St Helena in very good health. In the first year his health remained excellent. During his first two months, while at Briars Pavilion (and before the arrival of Hudson Lowe), he was allowed to walk into Jamestown and to mingle and talk (as best he could) with the townspeople.

This is not to suggest there was carelessness, far from it, the British kept a tight and disciplined watch on their prisoner and for any suggestion of a rescue bid. A constant lookout was kept for approaching ships which, once sighted, normally some 60 miles off, were announced by the firing of a gun, a reward given to the first man who spotted it. Some 500 guns were manned, sited around the island to prevent illicit landing or embarkation by small boat.

The transfer to Longwood brought with it isolation from the islanders and closer scrutiny by his gaolers. Longwood House and its grounds were enclosed by a wall four miles in circumference.

Within the grounds was the separate cottage at Hutt's Gate (about 100 metres from the main house) occupied by the Bertrand family. A modest but relatively private abode for the Imperial Grand Marshal.

The garrison at Deadwood Barracks provided 125 sentries to guard and watch over Longwood by day and 72 at night. In total on the island were some 2,280 troops, including 500 officers. At night a curfew was imposed. An officer was stationed at the house.

Napoleon took long walks and rides in the Longwood estate, accompanied at a short distance by a British officer. He objected to the close proximity of this officer (under standing orders to keep him in sight).When Lowe refused to budge, Napoleon ceased riding.

From early on the Emperor instructed that they should maintain distance between themselves, the Governor and other British authorities on the island. This was in any case, not difficult, as Sir Hudson Lowe was not to his taste.

Sir Hudson Lowe tried to be on good terms with his prisoner, but this approach was short-lived once he found his overtures rejected. The two could not bear to be in each other's company, exacerbated by the Governor's insistence on referring to Napoleon as "General Bonaparte".

Hudson Lowe, an experienced quartermaster, soon discovered that Napoleon's entourage enjoyed the finer things in life. Each day from Jamestown came fresh supplies of the best available meats, ducks, turkeys, etc. In fact, Napoleon's personal taste in food was simple for a man of his stature, but he provided for others as befitted him.

His preference was for Gevrey-Chambertin with a little water and for champagne. He developed a taste for Klein Constantia, a sweet yellowy dessert wine from Muscat grapes grown in the Cape.

Lowe concluded that the expenditure of the household, met by the British Government, was extortionate and cut the allowance. This further soured their infrequent meetings and correspondence, much of which reflected complaints from Napoleon about his living conditions and meagre allowance. The subject became a weapon to beat each other.

Two skirmishes highlighted the rift. Marchand, the Emperor's valet, visited a cobbler in Jamestown with a worn-out pair of his master's shoes to commission replacements. On receiving a report of this mundane matter, Lowe saw an opportunity to humiliate his adversary. The cobbler was forbidden to make the shoes without his express approval. Lowe visited "General Bonaparte", to tell him that if he wanted new shoes, he must make the request to him in person, presenting his own worn-out pair. Lowe would then make the necessary arrangements.

The erstwhile Emperor regarded him for a short time and said "you are sticking pins into us. You wish to prevent us escaping – there is only one way – to kill us."

Their short interview ended; Lowe was ushered out by General Bertrand. However much he sought to downplay formalities, Hudson Lowe found that he continued to be received as if he were attending a superior, in a microcosm of a court. He could not help resenting this. This jumped up, self-aggrandized tyrant had lost, but treated him like a supplicant, a junior granted an audience!

Exasperated, Lowe remarked to Bertrand that "I went to see General Bonaparte determined to be conciliatory. He created an imaginary Spain, an imaginary Poland. Now he wants to make an imaginary St Helena!"

Few of their captors had direct sight of or access to Napoleon. The Governor was the most dangerous, the one who could insist on access and proximity, would recognize change. They had to get under Lowe's skin and make his visits to Longwood as infrequent as strictly necessary, their duration a short perfunctory minimum.

Bonaparte's words were effective, but Lowe felt increasingly uneasy. These words did nothing to soothe his thoughts, as he returned to Jamestown and in the subsequent days.

The chances of his prisoner escaping were, or should be, near to nil, but this was the man who had turned the World on its head more than once, who escaped from Elba and reignited the flames.

The thought that he should be responsible were Bonaparte to escape was nerve-racking for a man of his serious disposition, his circumstances, a career army officer of no special background, privilege or sponsorship. He would be cashiered, held to account and ignominy by his superiors, his government, his nation, his King – a laughingstock in the eyes of the world, with nowhere to hide, his name forever tarnished, infamous – it was too dreadful to contemplate, except that he was forced to, by the nature of his charge – a man who had never been contained before.

Lowe ordered that the perimeter and sentry postings around Longwood be brought closer and that sentries on night duty must take up position in the garden at 6pm, instead of 9pm, as before.

The prisoner must feel his incarceration, hopelessness of rescue, of escape. If he would not behave he should understand there were consequences. The man of action who had been the master of his destiny and that of millions of others was a caged bird.

Lowe decided to go a step further, he insisted that the senior members of Napoleon's household each sign a written undertaking that, in exchange for being permitted to remain with General Bonaparte, they personally undertook not to leave the island other than in the event of his death or by the Governor's consent. Resentfully, they each did so. Lowe had correctly surmised they would not leave their master. If they were to begin do so it would set alarm bells ringing at Plantation House long before they could depart.

Lowe ruled that of the not infrequent gifts and packages that arrived on the island addressed to his prisoner from well-wishers, only those that made no reference to his former imperial status should be delivered. Only a minority got through. All were examined for hidden messages or other items.

Napoleon complained regularly "of all my privations, the most painful, the one I shall never get used to, is being parted from my wife and son."

Josephine had long been his passion, but in time, through absences and affairs, their relationship had cooled and, ever mindful of his legacy and need to cement the position of his family, his newly crowned imperial dynasty, after his victories had finally crushed the Austrians, the Emperor Francis had paid a high price to keep his throne.

In 1806, after a long series of campaigns between revolutionary France and the Holy Roman Empire, Napoleon forced the end of the empire that ruled much of Europe since Charlemagne was crowned in 800.

A humiliated and resentful Francis retained the status of Emperor of Austria. More fighting, more victories followed, until at Wagram in 1809 Napoleon himself inflicted a crushing defeat. The terms he exacted from Francis in Vienna under the Treaty of Schönbrunn were the toughest yet.

Hardest of all for Francis, head of the mighty and ancient Habsburg Dynasty, was to agree, at the initial suggestion of his own Foreign Minister, Count Metternich and after as much resistance as he could muster, to proposing a marriage between this upstart Corsican nemesis and his eldest daughter, Marie Louise, a great prize.

A prize Napoleon very nearly was unable to claim. While he stayed at Francis's Palace of Schönbrunn, overlooking Vienna, a young knife-wielding German assassin had only just been prevented from his lethal mission by the vigilance of one of his aides.

There were amazed reactions to these events. In France celebrations. In Britain, which continued to be at war with France, The Gentleman's Magazine commented "This Treaty is certainly one of the most singular documents in the annals of diplomacy. We see a Christian King, calling himself the father of his people, disposing of 400,000 of his subjects, like swine in a market. We see a great and powerful Prince condescending to treat with his adversary for the brushwood of his own forests. We see the hereditary claimant of the Imperial Sceptre of Germany not only condescending to the past innovations on his own dominions but assenting to any future alterations which the caprice or tyranny of his enemy may dictate with respect to his allies in Spain and Portugal, or to his neighbours in Italy. We see through the whole of this instrument the humiliation of the weak and unfortunate Francis, who has preferred the resignation of his fairest territories to restoring to his vassals their liberties and giving them that interest in the public cause which their valour would have known how to protect. O, the brave and loyal but, we fear, lost Tyrolese!"

Napoleon divorced Josephine and married his new bride with great pomp. He had planned strategically, dynastically, not expecting that he would fall in love with his new bride, who agreed to the marriage out of duty, prepared from childhood for an arranged match, though certainly not this one. Nevertheless, she knew her duty, her obligations to father and family, the lot of Habsburg daughters.

Napoleon relished the prospect of his bride to be. Reports and a portrait of Marie Louise told him she was young, fresh, charming, beautiful, alluring, altogether delightful in her inexperience. Everything Josephine could not offer. He was eager, the more so at the prospect of begetting the heir that he and Josephine had together failed to produce, to their mutual sadness. An heir essential to ambitions, to inherit his achievements. His recognition in the highest rank.

He showered her with gifts. A wonderful Parisian trousseau, diamonds and other jewels fit for his Empress. Napoleon sent his sister Caroline, Queen of Naples and Marshal Berthier his Chief of Staff to prepare the way. Berthier stood as his proxy at the wedding service held in Vienna. Caroline and Berthier spent a fortune on balls and fireworks. Vienna was alight, with dancing, operatic performances and galas.

Francis had genuine affection for his daughter. For an ostensibly stiff, aloof man, hidebound by the customs of his own court, he did all he knew how to soothe her nerves, to reassure her.

Finally, in a train of carriages, the young bride left Vienna behind to join him in France.

Never a patient man, he found it impossible to wait calmly for her in Paris. At heart he hoped for something more romantic than a political union. He insisted that her Austrian companions must leave her at the border with France - from there only her new French companions would travel with her on her daily progress toward Paris.

A fretful Napoleon could wait no more. He set out for the Chateau of Compiegne, some sixty kilometres from Paris, where they were to meet for the first time. He decided to press on. Fresh horses were harnessed to his carriage and, with night descending, in lashing rain, they pushed on to Soissons, where Marie Louise was due to dine. She had not arrived. On he went, into the night, with more fresh horses.

At Courcelles he met the outrider who foretold her imminent arrival. Soaked head to toe in water and mud, he waited, pacing in the doorway of the church. When the procession of sodden horses and coaches emerged, it was halted by one of his officers. The door of the carriage was opened, and Napoleon's presence heralded by a chamberlain. "L'Empereur!".

Napoleon entered the carriage. Behind the closed door he soon bestowed all of the pent-up passion and ardour of an impatient middle-aged man and conqueror upon his prize. He ordered there should be no stop at Soissons. They pressed on to Compiegne. There the couple had dinner, all dismissed, careful arrangements set aside.

More grand formalities of marriage and the coronation took place in Paris with great fanfare and pomp. He placed the newly minted crown of Empress on her head.

That first urgent overpowering devouring greeting set the tone for their relationship. He fell in love. She, overwhelmed, observed her duty.

Louise won her new husband's heart. He felt proud and protective of her, moved to tenderness. Soon she, thankfully, wonderfully, bore him the son, the heir, that he so badly needed, descended from among the noblest houses of Europe. This son, born in March 1811, Napoléon François Charles Joseph Bonaparte, styled the King of Rome, was his greatest treasure, heir to a new empire.

A new era of peace with Austria followed, his young wife loyally taking her husband's part, France's part, not always to the pleasure of her father or family, Count Metternich and other powerful players at her father's court.

As Napoleon now knew was a miscalculation, he had assumed, hoped, that family ties would bring Austria onto his side, as Louise loyally tried to bring about, or at least make it neutral in the wider European theatre.

Life was rarely so simple, and the rulers of Austria did not share this sentiment, long enmity with revolutionary France and memories of recent humiliations fresh. He might marry a Habsburg, under duress, but could never be accepted. They hated him the more for it, were that possible.

After his first abdication his wife and son returned to Vienna to her father. He wrote to her regularly from Elba, hoping for warm replies, for news, missing them profoundly, asking her to join him, to bring their boy. His letters were intercepted, falling into the hands of Metternich and Emperor Francis, who made it clear to her that she must not return to her husband, who was grieving for Josephine.

At Schönbrunn Louise rarely saw her father and stepmother. She had never felt secure in the belief that her husband's close relations with Josephine were not continued during her marriage. Napoleon had remained on good terms with his former wife and mistress and this insecurity was fed by reports from Francis's spies and other 'well-wishers'.

Once back in Paris, retaking the reins of power, Europe reawakening to the prospect of the renewal of conflict and upheaval, Napoleon had written urgently to his father-in-law. He sent his Minister of Foreign Affairs, the trusted Armand de Caulaincourt post haste to the Austrian Court to persuade them of his peaceful intentions, toward Austria and in general, with the private request for the return of his family and with the message that should he again have to abdicate, his son would reign under the regency of Louise.

He hoped that, tired of war, Austria and the other powers would prefer peace and, however reluctantly, accept the reality of his restored regime in France, a regime no longer threatening conflict and one the heir to which was half Habsburg.

Napoleon wrote to Louise that their apartments (maltreated during their recent enforced absence) were redecorated and that "all that is missing now, my good Louise, is you and my son. So, come and join me at once by way of Strasbourg."

Weeks later Napoleon received a blow he felt profoundly. He heard from Claude Méneval, just returned from Vienna a report that his wife had openly declared that she and his son would not be returning to Paris. He felt betrayed and deeply frustrated, angry and sad. He was well aware of the political and strategic significance of this clear physical statement to him, to France, to everyone. He was being snubbed, taunted and humiliated by Francis.

Méneval faithfully accompanied and served his master on his campaigns and travels and was present to witness many of the seminal events of his career. He accompanied Louise and the King of Rome on their difficult journey to Vienna in March and April 1814. To hide it from being looted by Cossacks he had broken the blade of the Emperor's sword with the Regent diamond affixed to its pommel and hidden it in his greatcoat.

He sent reports to his master on the meetings of the representatives of the Great Powers on the future of Europe and the comings and goings at the Congress. A whirl of balls, galas, concerts, operatic performances, theatrical and other entertainments, amid complex bedroom diplomacy, manoeuvrings and one-upmanship, featuring the Emperor, Tsar Alexander and other crowned heads, foreign ministers and ambassadors of nations great and small (and those hoping for revival), endless spies and hangers on.

These reports were delivered via the Carabelli brothers, merchants from an influential Corsican family. They assisted Napoleon and his family with many tasks, sharing heritage and customs, steeped in the history, the troubled and violent internecine quarrels of that colourful island.

Worse, the screw was turned by rumours, soundly based, of a blossoming relationship between his lonely wife and Count Adam Albert von Neipperg, a malevolent presence.

Neipperg was a handsome man of intrigue, adventures and misadventures that could only be guessed at, enhanced by a dramatic black bandage over his empty right eye socket, covering a wound received from a French sabre in a fiercely fought action as a younger man. A mature romantic figure, with a reputation as a soldier, diplomat, duellist and womaniser, a trail of conquests in his wake.

Years earlier, when Neipperg was attached to the Austrian Embassy in Paris, Napoleon had sought to win him over, awarding him the golden eagle of the Legion d'Honneur.

This ambitious, unscrupulous, indomitably anti-French and anti-Bonapartist, Austrian aristocrat and army officer had become a confidant and agent of Count Metternich. Metternich was pleased to observe a mutual affinity when the French Empress and Neipperg were introduced on the glittering occasion of the meeting of the two Emperors at Dresden in May 1812, her husband at the zenith of his power, surrounded by those kings and princes whom he had made into his vassals or even appointed.

Metternich had long-since recognised the usefulness of Neipperg. He was sent to neutral Sweden as Ambassador. Due to the lack of an heir from his old dynasty and seeking stability in the royal succession, in 1810 the King, Charles XIII and the Swedish Parliament (Riksdag) had chosen an heir presumptive whom it was thought would meet with the approval of the then de facto ruler of Europe, Napoleon - Jean Baptiste Jules Bernadotte. Having learned that relations between the two men were not as warm as supposed, it was Neipperg's secret and successful mission, as events bore out, to encourage the separation of strategically influential Sweden from the Bonapartist cause.

He was kept busy, criss-crossing Europe (overthrowing Murat in Naples, elsewhere persuading allies to abandon Napoleon's cause), stirring up problems.

Neipperg's ruthlessness extended to the treatment of lovers. He was known to have swept his married Italian lover, Teresa Pola off her feet, persuaded her to leave her cuckolded husband, and then, she having borne him five children, to have married her in order to legitimise them. This inconvenience was not allowed to get in the way of his new mission.

As Napoleon now suspected, Louise's return to Vienna in 1814 was a decisive step in a larger plan to separate him from his wife and his son. Francis and Metternich would prevent their return to him. Neipperg's role was to be Louise's chaperone, guard and mentor. If something more romantic were to ensue, while scandalous, it would serve to drive a wedge between her and Napoleon from which there could be no return. A final insult to him, to his honour and to that of France!

Neipperg was instructed by Metternich to accompany Louise, then at Aix-les-Bains, to keep her entertained and to prevent her from joining her husband on Elba. Abandoning the devoted Teresa Pola, he assumed the role with relish.

He had licence to woo a young and attractive Habsburg princess and empress, the wife of his arch enemy. He resolved to himself that within six months they would be lovers and that he would in time make her his wife. He was not the type to be put off by impediments.

Louise set off with her new constant companion on a tour of Munich, Baden and Geneva. This was a vacation, a distraction for a young woman who had recently experienced great events. Undisturbed by messages from her husband (intercepted by her Father's secret service), in romantic surroundings, Louise was soon enjoying the attention paid to her by the dashing Neipperg.

He would sing to her when they were alone in the evenings. Theirs became an enduring relationship.

News of their closeness spread, causing offence and upset in France and in Austria. The honour of both countries impugned.

Méneval reported on this affair at first hand, worse he brought with him a message: "I hope he will understand the misery of my position...I shall never assent to a divorce, but I flatter myself that he will not oppose an amicable separation, and that he will not bear any ill feeling towards me... This separation has become imperative; it will in no way affect the feelings of esteem and gratitude that I preserve." Their personal relationship was ended, she was his wife in name, the mother of his beloved son and heir and a significant piece on the chessboard.

He knew her to be shy, timid and persuadable, in the manipulative hands of his enemies. It had been an affair of state, not a love match. He did not feel enmity; she had wanted to accompany him to Elba. It was he who had sent her to her father, to intercede for him and their son, hoping to preserve the Empire for his heir.

He was sustained by words etched into his memory. Méneval reported that when, before leaving Vienna, he took his leave of Louise and the King of Rome, saying to the boy: "I am going to see your father. Do you have anything to say to him?". The young prince had replied sadly: "Monsieur Méva, please tell him that I still love him a lot".

News reached him that the Congress had, as a final act, appointed the 24 year-old Louise as Duchess of Parma, where now she ruled with her ever-present companion, Count Neipperg. He did not begrudge her happiness.

His son had been held in Vienna, in effect a hostage, no longer styled the King of Rome but dubbed Duke of Reichstadt.

It was not lost on him that Louise would be freed to marry by his death. A tidy solution for his Austrian enemies!

Freedom comes at a price, he mused.

What most upset him, these thousands of miles away, was that he could not see his son, share in his upbringing, could not teach him all he would need to know, all he should impart to him, his heir.

Worse, brought up at the Austrian Court, surrounded by enemies, the boy was being alienated from his father, his family and his country, his destiny denied, stolen or destroyed. His education and circumstances designed to ensure he could not follow in his father's footsteps.

Francis and Metternich had a knife in their hands to twist and they did.

From the firm of Beaggini in Italy he received the gift of a marble bust of the boy. Lowe had initially confiscated it, because it was not sent openly, he worried that it might contain a message, but reluctantly he allowed it to be delivered for fear of negative publicity. Napoleon had it placed in his bedroom and pointed it out with pride to visitors.

Albine de Montholon was delivered of her fourth child in June 1816, a daughter, who was named Napoléone Marie Hélène Charlotte. She soon bore a striking resemblance to the Emperor and rumours spread.

Many factors contribute to success or failure in a campaign or battle. None knew better. There could only be one attempt.

Amongst the greatest challenges was to develop a reliable, trustworthy and secure means of communication with those who would help them. The time it took to exchange messages was frustratingly long and imposed limitations.

The English were fully alert to the certainty that there would be attempts at secret communication. Everything and everyone that came from or was destined for Longwood and its residents was meticulously examined or searched.

Before leaving France Napoleon made arrangements for messages, sent by a variety of correspondents, including family members and some of his former aides and supporters, to be delivered to him, wherever he would end up, by different methods, arriving in packages, dressed up in varying guises, through the post and cargo addressed to him and his companions. Finding such items would keep his captors busy and would go some way to satisfying them of the effectiveness of their scrutiny. Messages discovered could serve to misdirect and unsettle Lowe.

Communication there was. 'Real' coded messages and his instructions confirmed by the inclusion of a key word, pre-agreed with Schulmeister and known only to the very few most trusted persons in their circle, including Joseph. A system they had long used to conduct their most private affairs.

For secure delivery they selected a reliable and regular method. False-bottomed casks of wine, with a thin hidden chamber, packed solid, which did not echo a tell-tale hollow sound when tapped by the English sentinels. The substantial consumption by the Longwood household and its regular orders for French and Italian foodstuffs, wines and other goods required a constant supply, consigned from Genoa and Marseilles, carried by merchant ships. Coded orders sent outwards, concealed letters returned, the emptied barrels, their contents consumed, chopped up and used for firewood. Simple, but effective.

As a 'disaffected' Gourgaud would later confirm to Lowe over dinner at his table, before departing the island, Dr. O'Meara had operated as a conduit, as did British merchant naval officers, willing to accept reward. Some of these communications were intercepted, as anticipated.

Schulmeister was a renowned master of disguises and a consummate actor. He first met Napoleon in 1804 in Strasbourg, in the Great Hall, where he asked to be employed as an agent. When asked for references, he had replied "Sire, I have no recommendations but my own", to which the reply was "you may go. We have no work for men without references" and Napoleon departed behind a screen. Schulmeister adjusted his dress, puckered his face and, when the Emperor came back, he thought he was interviewing a different candidate. In reply to Napoleon's demand of "who are you?" he replied "I am Karl Schulmeister. You interviewed me a moment ago. Now that I have demonstrated my ability to change my personality completely, perhaps you could find me a job in your service?"

Within a year the French took Vienna and he was made Commissioner of Police. Napoleon would come to say that Schulmeister was worth an army division.

There were many tales of Schulmeister's seemingly impossible exploits. As a secret courier of a letter from one of Napoleon's Ministers to a spy in the Austrian Army, Schulmeister disguised himself as a jewel merchant. He was arrested and searched by the Austrians. The letter was found and he was sentenced to be shot the following dawn. He was guarded by six Austrian soldiers. When wine was brought to them, he managed to introduce opium that he had hidden in his clothes. He donned one of their uniforms, found the person the message was intended for and recited it to him word for word from memory, before making his escape through Austrian and French army lines.

On another occasion, at the Battle of Wagram, he was pursued into a house by Austrian soldiers. As the Austrians burst into the house, they were met by a barber coming down the stairs with razors, soap and towels. The Austrians demanded "we are chasing a spy, have you seen him?", to which the reply was "a man ran upstairs". The soldiers ran upstairs. Schulmeister made himself scarce.

Napoleon was served well and enjoyed hearing of his spymaster's exploits. He did the seemingly impossible with incredible audacity.

Schulmeister managed to attend an Austrian Council of War, dressed as an Austrian general, in place of the true general whom he had bribed with one million francs. Emperor Ferdinand, overseeing the meeting, did not spot the fraud. The debate was reported by Schulmeister in person to Napoleon.

He achieved something even more remarkable, presenting himself to Marshal Karl Freiherr Mack von Leiberich, Commander of the Austrian Army, declaring himself a Hungarian nobleman who had lived in France for many years, now banished on suspicion of being an Austrian spy. He asked to be allowed to exact revenge by truly becoming a spy for the Austrians. Mack arranged a commission for him, got him in as a member of the leading military clubs in Vienna and appointed him chief of intelligence on his own staff.

One day he entered Mack's office bearing a French newspaper and saying that "we have just had news that the French are about to revolt against the tyrant Bonaparte. Most of their army is being withdrawn from our border to deal with the expected uprising". Setting the newspaper on Mack's desk, he added "this was smuggled from France. You will see it says civil strife is spreading across the country. This confirms information from our spies. France will soon be torn by civil war". Mack grasped the situation quickly – "this is the time to attack, when the French are at their weakest!" He ordered the advance of his 30,000 strong army to Ulm, there he was surrounded by a much stronger French Army under Napoleon and obliged to surrender. Taken prisoner by the French, Schulmeister was 'interrogated' by Napoleon, made his escape and got back to Vienna, continuing as Director of Intelligence for the Austrians.

Schulmeister supplied his French master with a steady stream of information on the movements and condition of the Austrian forces, contributing to their defeat at the decisive battle at Austerlitz.

Suspicions circulated and he was in danger of exposure. An order was issued for his arrest. He was rescued just in time by French forces under Joachim Murat that overran Vienna.[vi]

In 1816 three Allied Commissioners landed in Jamestown tasked with seeing that Napoleon was safely secured there, which they confirmed to their masters.

It was obvious that their exfiltration would have to be drawn out, with no discernible pattern. Nothing could alert their captors to optimistic changes of circumstance.

Elements of their plans and instructions needed to be relayed. They could not be set down in writing. One of them must prepare the way. Las Cases was chosen. The others did not demur. Neither de Montholon nor Gourgaud, especially, would miss him. And he would take his son, who was fretting.

A contrivance secured Las Cases' expulsion by an indignant Sir Hudson Lowe who had had him arrested on 25 November 1816 for attempting to smuggle out a letter from Napoleon. Lowe told Las Cases that he would permit him to remain provided he met conditions, which he refused. Lowe ordered him off the island. He was shipped to Cape Town, thence, after a delay, to Europe.

Barred from entering France by the government of Louis XVIII, he made his way to Brussels. It was there that Schulmeister's agent found and debriefed him. Confirmation of his arrival reached Longwood.

Schulmeister's fortunes had seen dramatic changes. The Austrians took revenge on his properties in 1814, though he managed to evade capture and probable execution. Thrown into prison by the Prussians after Waterloo, he paid a huge sum for his release. Back in France he knew he was followed and watched everywhere, limiting his freedom of movement, necessitating constant watchfulness, subterfuge and the selective employment of trusted (well rewarded and therefore expensive) lieutenants.[vii]

In 1817 Joseph Bonaparte[viii]embarked for the United States. There he sold jewels and installed himself in New York and Philadelphia. His home became a magnet for French emigres and Francophiles.

Lawyer, politician and diplomat, experienced in dealing with the Americans, Joseph was to negotiate for his brother to be permitted to come to live in quiet retirement.

There was no appetite amongst the Americans to house a man who would upset relations with the major powers. Lavish entertainment accompanied by eloquent persuasion and substantial offers of money could not sway the decision. Joseph remained in America, acquiring an estate at Point Breeze, Bordentown, New Jersey, where he received many figures of the day.

On St Helena relations between the chief gaoler and his prisoner remained frosty. Bonaparte was much the stronger character and intellect, able to play the cat with this mouse, made easier by his adversary's fear of losing his prisoner.

Lowe had taken to visiting Longwood on surprise inspections, testing its security. He was doing just this one afternoon when he came across an islander, of Indian origin, about in the grounds. It was explained he had been hired as a servant to Napoleon. Lowe had him arrested and dismissed.

Lowe's mood was not improved by Napoleon's obvious friendliness toward other British officers and their families. Napoleon held long and friendly conversations with Admiral Malcolm, who had arrived to take over the Naval contingent. He played chess with Lady Malcolm.

Lowe took Malcolm with him to visit Napoleon, so that he might see for himself how he was treated by the Frenchman. Lowe returned to a bête noir – household expenses, informing Napoleon that these were too high. He said that he had tried to deal on the matter with Bertrand, who had declined to discuss it, out of disrespect.

After a long silence, Napoleon addressed Admiral Malcolm: "General Bertrand is a man who commanded armies, and he treats him like a corporal… He treats us all like deserters from the Royal Corsican Regiment. He's been sent out as a hangman. General Bertrand doesn't want to see him. None of us do. We would rather have four days of bread and water." Shocked and angered, Lowe replied "I am perfectly indifferent to all this. I did not seek this job - it was offered to me and I considered it a sacred duty to accept it." Napoleon replied, "then if the order were given to you to assassinate me you would accept it?' "No Sir" replied Lowe.

Lowe then said money must be saved and so supplies would be reduced. Napoleon replied "who asked you to feed me? Do you see the camp there, where the troops are? I shall go there and say, "the oldest soldier in Europe begs to join your mess" and share their dinner."

Napoleon accused Lowe of reflecting the blind hatred of his master, Lord Bathurst, the Colonial Secretary. Lowe exclaimed "Lord Bathurst, sir, does not know what blind hatred is!"

Napoleon continued "I am Emperor. When England and Europe are gone, when your name and Lord Bathurst's are forgotten, I shall still be the Emperor Napoleon. You had no right to put [Bertrand] under house arrest – you never commanded armies – you were nothing but a staff officer. I had imagined I should be well treated among the English, but you are not an Englishman!"

Lowe replied tersely "you make me smile sir". "How smile?" Napoleon replied. "Yes sir, you force me to smile – your misconception of my character and the rudeness of your manners excite my pity – I wish you good day!" Lowe walked out.

Lowe followed up on this heated exchange by making the security arrangements even more visible from Longwood – posting sentries in plain view - and informing General Bonaparte that His Britannic Majesty's Government's contribution to Longwood's expenditure on provisions (running at some £20,000 per year – a huge sum) must reduce to £1,000 per month, with any difference paid for by the French. Lowe confirmed this in person to de Montholon, when he told him that French Government funds were used up and they would have to foot any extra themselves.

Marchand and Cipriani were despatched to Jamestown on three occasions with large baskets full of the Emperor's table silver, which they were to break up, removing all symbols first. The substantial hoard was sold in plain view to Gideon Solomon, a Jamestown jeweller. Sailors, officers and merchants bound for England and elsewhere saw this and asked for an explanation. Sir Hudson Lowe, whom, having heard of this event had gone to investigate, challenged Cipriani to explain "why do you need so much money?" "To buy food, Excellency" came the reply. Napoleon let it be known that "the next thing I must sell will be my clothes!"

December and January witnessed visibly deteriorating relations between Gourgaud and the de Montholons and between Gourgaud and Napoleon. These persisted into 1817 and were reported to Lowe.

Ostensibly because he resented the required constant presence of a British officer, Napoleon ceased to ride and began to remain in or close to the house. The man who had been seen to arrive on the island in rude good health seemed to be suffering from the damp and cold prevalent on the Deadwood Plateau.

One regular visitor to Longwood was always admitted. Betsy Balcombe had become a firm friend. He was charmed by her inquisitiveness, her playful innocence. She was fascinated by this man of great charm, vast experience and twinkling eyes. Often Cipriani would prepare for her a treat and she was a favourite amongst the household, bringing good cheer.

Reports in Europe, newspapers, still speculated about an affair, but this was untrue. Friendship and joy in each other's company is possible between the most apparently unlikely and unequal of partners.

Betsy's father had done very well as procurer and supplier in chief to Longwood's residents, in effect 'By Appointment...'.

The comings and goings of the Balcombe's excited the suspicion of Lowe and others. Perhaps there was jealousy over the obviously warm and friendly relations. Suspecting secret messages were passing between Longwood and the outside world, Lowe concluded that the Balcombes must be involved. He intervened to cause William Balcombe's dismissal by the East India Company and removal from the island.

Their leave taking in March 1818 was sad, all knowing they would not meet again. Betsy's and her parents' departure removed familiar sources of amusement, friendly faces.

Another regular intimate at Longwood was Barry O'Meara, who looked after the health of the Prisoner and his entourage. It might have been expected that O'Meara would become the most effective of spies and rapporteurs in the employ of the British, but that is not how things turned out. In practice O'Meara was placed in a very awkward spot. As a doctor he owed care and confidentiality to his patient, as a servant of the British Crown he owed fealty.

Lowe, a fellow Irishman, expected to find a willing friend and agent ready to report on all he found and observed during his regular visits and examinations.

The occupants of Longwood, especially Napoleon, impressed upon him the importance of reporting to the Admiralty and to the outside world the poor and unhealthy conditions and climate at Longwood and the negative impact these were having on the Prisoner's health.

The stated objective was to garner public sympathy and political pressure in Europe, especially in London, to demand Bonaparte's return to Europe for the sake of his health. Press reports, encouraged by Bonapartists, including Napoleon's family, supported in England by liberals such as Lord Byron, the poet, were emphasising the poor climate, poor quality of food and risk of tropical diseases.

Lowe discovered that O'Meara was corresponding with a well-placed friend at the Admiralty, John Finlaison, who was passing these letters to his superiors, including the Secretary at the Admiralty and Lord Melville. They described matters concerning Napoleon and Lowe. He decided to be rid of O'Meara.

By early 1818 relations between Lowe and O'Meara – who had found himself intolerably squeezed between the French and British contingents – were breaking down entirely, O'Meara refusing to cooperate. It was clear to Lowe that O'Meara had been suborned by Boney and was now useless, dangerous and probably actively conspiring to help his prisoner. He also suspected him of facilitating communication between Longwood and the outside world.

O'Meara offered his resignation, which was refused. Lowe feared a trap and knew that London had to be squared first.

At Longwood the complement grew by the addition of yet another baby daughter born to Albine de Montholon.

Gaspard Gourgaud was the next to leave. A simmering and visible disagreement with de Montholon, treated as his superior (a cause of actual irritation to him in their confined world), an exchange of 'intolerable' insults and a challenge to a duel, satisfaction demanded. The Emperor stepped in, issuing rebukes.

Gourgaud requested an urgent audience with Sir Hudson Lowe. He made it clear his relationship with de Montholon had broken down irretrievably.

A duel could not be allowed. Newspapers at home and across Europe would have a field day and Lowe was left even more certain in his belief that Bonaparte was masquerading ill health and conducting a propaganda campaign, in which O'Meara was complicit, and should stay put at Longwood.

In early February 1818 Gourgaud submitted a letter to Napoleon seeking to be relieved of his duties, citing ill-health. He received a written confirmation and an award of a pension of 12,000 Francs for life.

The next day, 13 February, he departed Longwood, with Lowe's permission, and moved into Bayle Cottage, near Plantation House, together with Lieutenant Basil Jackson (also a veteran of Waterloo). The two had come to know one another as Jackson had been tasked with overseeing repairs at Longwood. Jackson had seen the ill-feelings at work at Longwood with his own eyes and confirmed as much to Lowe.

That evening they dined as Sir Hudson Lowe's guests. Lowe was a solicitous host, but he asked Gourgaud point blank whether he was on a mission for Napoleon and whether, if he were to search him and his belongings, he would find anything of importance? Gourgaud assured him he would not.

The next day Lowe instructed his military secretary, Major Gorrequer, to examine Gourgaud's papers and belongings. This was done in Jackson's presence. Nothing was found.

Jackson remained close to Gourgaud until he left the island. They dined regularly at Plantation House. Perhaps Lowe hoped Gourgaud would let something slip. One evening he confirmed it had been easy to exchange letters with correspondents in England and O'Meara was implicated. Another evening revealed that Napoleon had had to be persuaded not to commit suicide, as he had threatened more than once.

Lowe took comfort his prisoner considered his situation hopeless. He concluded Gourgaud was "a foolish, vain fellow, without sense enough to conceal his weaknesses" and loaned him one hundred pounds from his own funds.

Before Gourgaud departed St Helena, Baron Sturmer, the Austrian Commissioner, there to observe the prisoner and keep Metternich and his Emperor informed, who lived near to Bayle Cottage, invited the General to see him. Asked by Sturmer whether Napoleon spoke of his future? Gourgaud replied (as Sturmer reported and Gourgaud recorded) "He is convinced that he will not stay at St Helena." Sturmer asked "Do you think he can escape?", to which Gourgaud said "He has had the opportunity ten times, and he still has it at this moment." The startled Sturmer commented "I confess that does not seem impossible", to which Gourgaud responded "What is not possible when one has millions at his disposal? He can escape alone and go to America whenever he wishes."

Another member of the household was to leave. The cook, Michel Lepage who had married Jeanette, a Belgian who previously worked at Plantation House. The couple left St Helena in May 1818. The remaining residents of Longwood ate Chinese food (to Lowe's amusement) until replacements could be sent from Europe.

Gourgaud arrived in London in early May 1818 and was taken to see Henry Goulburn, the Under-Secretary of State for War and the Colonies, a deputy to Lord Bathurst, for 'de-briefing'. He left two impressions. Bonaparte was in good health (better than reported) and

O'Meara, William Balcombe and some other Britons who had visited him were involved in furthering secret correspondence between Longwood and Europe. This meeting sealed O'Meara's fate. Lord Bathurst wrote forthwith to Lowe instructing him to expel O'Meara. O'Meara was ordered to leave Longwood on the day this letter arrived, 25 July 1818. He was arrested and put aboard a ship.

Gourgaud came across the French Ambassador, Marquis d'Osmond, to whom he declared it was possible for Napoleon to escape. When the Ambassador replied, "easily said", the General said "no, easily done and in all kinds of ways. Supposing for instance, that Napoleon were placed in one of the barrels that are sent to Longwood full of provisions and returned to Jamestown every day without being inspected. Do you believe it impossible to find a captain of a craft who for a bribe of one million francs would undertake to carry the barrel on board a vessel ready to sail?"

The Ambassador was entitled to assume that one so close to the subject would sow uncertainty and insecurity among his enemies. It was well known that at Rochefort, when it would have been easier to get away amid the aftermath of Waterloo and the prevailing disarray, Bonaparte had disdained a proposal to be hidden in a specially made cask and loaded onto a Danish vessel, on the grounds it did not befit his Imperial Dignity. A cause of mirth in the royalist circle in Paris! He could not simply embark as the 'dignified' former self-styled

Emperor of France, but as a hidden or disguised fugitive. Surely his impossible vanity would imprison him!

Gourgaud was vocally anti-Napoleon, but when the British authorities intercepted a letter from him to Empress Louise in which he wrote of her husband as a martyr in his remote and bleak place of exile, they decided he had fooled them. He was seized and shipped to Hamburg in November 1818. There he remained until he was allowed to return to France in 1821.

He received 12,000 Francs from Napoleon's brother, Eugene, as Napoleon promised.

Gourgaud fulfilled other aspects of his mission. More letters were written to the Emperors of Austria and Russia and to Louise, falling on deaf ears. Suggestive of the increasing desperation of their captive.[ix]

On a number of occasions Napoleon was heard to say that he regarded his prospects of escape as five out of a hundred. There were always rumours, on the island and elsewhere. There were plots too – some serious ones uncovered by the British authorities, whose network of agents and others currying favour or reward was extensive. Rumours emanated from the Americas, where there existed pockets of sympathy for the captive former Emperor and where Joseph Bonaparte plotted his brother's freedom, the Allies' intelligence services reported.

Opinions took the view that if Napoleon were to escape it would be to a new life in the Americas, where he could expect a warm welcome. Many of his former officers and supporters had found sanctuary there. All of this rumour and activity served to create a febrile atmosphere of anticipation. Could he, when, how, where would he go? Even in exile across the World this man continued to fascinate. It was impossible to ignore him.

After the departures of the Balcombes and O'Meara's forced exit from Longwood, Napoleon's absences from view became regular. British officers were instructed to peep and listen in, in the hope of seeing or hearing their prisoner, who was too ill to show himself. No British officer or official had seen him at close quarter - with the result that an apprehensive Lowe visited Longwood, demanding to see the prisoner. Lowe, uncharacteristically, accepted an assurance from de Montholon that the prisoner was still there. At one point the Emperor was not seen for two months.

An officer posted to Longwood was given orders to see General Bonaparte twice each day with his own eyes and report his presence, confirmed by telegraph to Sir Hudson Lowe. The Prisoner would have the shutters drawn and observe the officer through a telescope. One resourceful officer returned the compliment, using a telescope himself. Another mindful of his duty, crept up to the window for a peep inside. There he saw the Ogre in his bath and, when spotted, provoked the naked bather to charge at the door. The hapless officer turned tail and ran in full retreat!

Years earlier Schulmeister had offered to Napoleon a stratagem that confused his enemies and helped to maintain the morale of his troops. It was a simple effective deceit. The employment of doubles, a small, handpicked number of chosen men, trained to affect the Emperor's stances and mannerisms and whose appearance, when dressed suitably and put in the right context, could convince those who were not from the Emperor's immediate circle that he was present.

These men were rewarded for their loyalty and silence, but it was dangerous work. One 'Napoleon' had been shot dead, one was crippled after a riding accident and a third was poisoned before the Battle at Waterloo, victim of an assassination attempt.

Francois Eugene Robeaud assumed his peculiar services would no longer be in demand after Waterloo. It was difficult to hide from Schulmeister, however, and there was always the question of funds. Loyalty was important, money was a necessity – and Schulmeister had funds at his disposal. When the instructions came, Schulmeister knew whom to summon. A man who could be the Emperor in the eyes of all but those who knew him best, who had been tested in this deception many times before, totally trustworthy, known to Napoleon, and willing to swap his existence for that of the life prisoner on St Helena.

Robeaud, was found at home living with his sister at Baleycourt, near Verdun in North East France, tending his plot. He readily agreed. Such conditions might be intolerable for an emperor, but they held attractions for an ordinary man of the people who had discovered that his greatest asset was his capacity to be, for a time, a convincing mimic of a colossus. The benefits provided for the former Emperor of France would be a much better alternative to the uncertain future in the new France he could otherwise look forward to. Besides, he had enjoyed masquerading as an emperor, so surely, he would enjoy being an ex-emperor also?

He explained to her that he would be away on a secret mission and that they must move to Tours, in the Val de Loire, where he installed her (used to his comings and goings, minimal explanations). She was to receive a regular income and knew not to question Good Fortune. If asked, she would say he had gone away to sea.

Flight

The crew was a mixture of Frenchmen, Genoese, Sicilians, a handful of Corsicans, Spanish, Portuguese and even a few Irish. A tight-knit group.

Trade and survival in seas and coasts frequented by occasional pirates and others willing to take what they could, to whom life was cheap, required peculiar resourcefulness. The master, Pietro Mariani, was a short solid seafarer used to handling those who chose a life at sea and his command, owned by a Genoese mercantile house, associates of the Carabellis.

Shortly before they set sail on the outward leg of their regular voyage, the Capitano welcomed aboard Signor Bianchi, a supervisor and agent for the owners. He would observe their route and assess opportunities at the ports they were to visit and report. He should form a good impression.

The crew became used to his detachment, though one feature provoked humorous comment. An uncanny resemblance. Inevitable jokes wore thin. There was plenty to keep them occupied.

Bianchi berthed in the Capitano's cabin (who had bumped down the First Officer, and so on). On deck he stood alone, observing, lost in thought. He ate alone, though sometimes the Capitano joined him. When they stopped along the route he went ashore alone.

An old adage is that merchant ships must keep moving. A good master, and the Capitano was such a one, sticks to his schedule as best as conditions allow. Time spent idly wastes money and with the owner's agent aboard it was clear no time was to be wasted on this trip.

That suited the crew. Once they were into the South Atlantic the only port where they could find pleasure was Cape Town.

Jamestown was good for stretching legs ashore, a long evening at a tavern and a square meal of fresh food, but little else. Not a place to dwell. It was the Bonaventura's practice, weather and wind permitting, to spend no more than one or two nights there, offloading and loading cargoes, water and fresh provisions, before beginning the return leg.

The substantial consumption of wines had not only been noted by Sir Hudson Lowe, it also was the subject of ribald comment and envy among the garrison. Each month a wagon would stop by the jetty at Jamestown to be loaded, under the watchful gaze of a British officer. The quantities of fine wines in casks or bottled, champagne and other fine goods were impressive. This was the pattern. The officer on duty was well aware of his responsibility to ensure that this commerce did not conceal messages or other contraband.

Lowe might come to observe proceedings and poke around, nurturing his irritation at the largesse. Never before had a prisoner of war been allowed so much luxury!

Through Balcombe a channel had developed, sourcing from Italy, France and Gibraltar. The Bonaventura beat a route from Genoa, via Marseilles and Gibraltar, down the West coast of Africa, with port visits to drop off and collect cargoes and occasional passengers, thence to Cape Town and on to Jamestown, returning to repeat the exercise.

By August 1818 this route was familiar to all participants and observers, including British sentinels. Nothing occurred to cause the authorities to close off this supply of harmless, if expensive, cargo which would, Sir Hudson Lowe and Lord Bathurst knew, provoke outrage.

All visitors to Longwood, all vehicles, all goods delivered there were vetted by guards. They knew all regular visitors by sight, those members of the household who were permitted to come and go, to visit Jamestown. Frequent among these were Napoleon's valet Marchand

and, until shortly before his death in February 1818, the Maitre d'hotel Cipriani, the cook Michel Lepage, often accompanied by Jeanette.

Cipriani would check and sign for consignments by the dockside in Jamestown. Sailors from the Bonaventura would load them under watchful eyes onto wagons. They would return to Longwood accompanied by a Sergeant and a pair of soldiers from its garrison, for whom this domestic process relieved the boredom of routine.

The death of Cipriani and the departures of the Lepages necessitated changes. It became Marchand's duty to ride into Jamestown, accompanied by the 'temporary' Chinese cook, who would step off to find meat, fruit, vegetables and other household requirements. Having observed Cipriani on these missions it was an easy substitution. Marchand enjoyed his new responsibilities.

To the amusement of the British subalterns who oversaw these events, Marchand considered himself something of an expert 'nose'. Twice, having insisted on tapping the casks of wine awaiting loading onto his wagons, to the evident impatience of Mariani, he denounced a cask as 'off', refusing delivery. The Capitano, having tried the wines himself, vocally disputed this, to no avail. Marchand would not budge and the Capitano would not throw away the contents. The casks were reloaded, to be used for the crew's allowance.

Today Marchand was in a hurry. He must get back to Longwood. They were short-handed, the Emperor was in a bad temper and had insisted.

The casks were examined by guards for hidden contents, knocked for echoes, but the anticipated tasting did not take place. Mariani teased "so finally you accept I am right!". The reply was short "don't you worry, you may be certain I will let you know if there is a problem – you have the nose of an ass and the palate of a goat!" and with that the wagons set off with alacrity. They enjoyed their duel.

The next day Marchand pointed out to the duty officer that their Chinese cook had not been able to accompany him the day before, they were out of provisions and, what's more, three of the casks needed to be returned. The wine must have suffered in transit and was off. One barrel could perhaps be forgiven until the next occasion, three could not. He would make this abundantly clear to Mariani!

A wagon, Marchand, the Chinese cook, a Sergeant and two privates left for Jamestown within the hour.

Quite a scene unfolded at the dockside, the excitable French valet and the normally implacable ship's captain exchanging sharp words in a combination of French and Italian, watched by a British subaltern, a Sergeant and two amused privates, passing citizens of Jamestown, assorted Naval personnel and, until he peeled away to fulfil his tasks, a Chinese cook. There was elaborate tasting, with diametrically opposed conclusions. The outcome was that three barrels, their contents having been offered for independent tasting to the British officer and declined, were reloaded aboard the Bonaventura. Within the hour she went with the tide.

Painful memories of the rebellion of the American colonials, humiliating defeat of the British Army, were recent. The arrival of an American merchant vessel had created a stir. Reactions were mixed, curiosity from the indigenous population, outright hostility and suspicion from the garrison, not least the Governor.

On hearing of the arrival of the "Pride of Charleston", Lowe came to see for himself.

Watchers were positioned at vantage points, told to report anything unusual, anyone other than the crew going on board. No-one from Longwood was permitted near the vessel.

Henry Graham was summoned to meet Lowe. Asked to state his business in St Helena, Graham explained he had been instructed by his owners to investigate possibilities for using Jamestown as a stopping point, for provisioning and light repairs, a safe harbour against Atlantic storms, if necessary. Lowe doubted this plausible answer was the full story, knowing he could not extract more, without cause. He replied "well, Captain, I imagine our friends of the East India Company will take great interest in your plans. You must know that you are unlikely to be made welcome. My interest is in ensuring the peace and governance of this island and, as you must be aware, the security of my prisoner here. My eyes are on you and your crew. Behave yourselves, or I will know, and I will do my duty, whatever that requires."

Lowe relayed his conversation to Admiral Malcolm. The Royal Navy would escort the Pride out of St Helena's waters. It was only two years since a captain of an East India Company vessel had reported sighting an American vessel, a schooner, apparently holding station off St Helena. When approached by warships she had put on an impressive turn of speed and outrun them, again taking up station before leaving without explanation. Another American ship, a rare thing in these waters, had put into Jamestown harbour pleading shortage of fresh water. A dubious excuse, Lowe reported in despatches.

Aboard Bonaventura, Signor Bianchi, who had been unwell with a migraine during their visit to Jamestown, felt well enough to emerge to take air on deck that night and at intervals during the following day.

They toasted Marchand. What can you expect from a valet!

The Pride sailed one day after its arrival, there having been no disturbance, no reports of untoward comings or goings. Lowe was relieved, left with a nagging concern.

The Prisoner had taken to his bedroom, unwell again, and would see only Bertrand and Marchand for days. The telegraph signalled to Plantation House that Bonaparte was at Longwood.

That Autumn an indiscreet Mme Bertrand wrote in a letter to a friend "Success! Napoleon has left the island!"

Verona

Straddling the River Adige, Verona was once more under the Austrians after the fall of the French Empire, when it was part of Joseph Bonaparte's Kingdom of Italy, carved out by his brother.

Since ancient times it has been at the junction of important cross-roads. Its Roman amphitheatre and fine buildings, many paid for by rich merchants of the City, make it a characterful and comfortable place to live and to visit.

That the Veronese merchant Signor Petrucci took on a partner, Signor Revard, newly arrived from Genoa, a merchant and occasional dealer in diamonds and other precious stones, was interesting to his rivals, but unremarkable. In any event Revard, who so resembled old images of that famous Corsican now imprisoned on St Helena that his neighbours were amused to call him "Napoleon", was a quiet, friendly soul who went about his business quietly, politely, with a ready joke, playful gesture or smile if teased about his ridiculous resemblance to the famous man. He spoke excellent Italian, with an accent and soon settled. Those who dealt in these things found that the process of negotiating a sale was handled by Petrucci. Presumably Revard was the silent partner, the buyer, and his occasional absences must be for this purpose.

Signor Revard hired a cook and housekeeper, a cheerful woman, and a valet. Those of a prurient disposition speculated that the relationship between the attractive housekeeper and the still handsome, personable (and rich) widower were more than commercial.

The Valley of the Willows

The Emperor rallied.

He developed a determined and surprising interest in gardening, in particular in growing vegetables in the grounds of Longwood beside the house. This outdoor activity was more appreciated by his captors than by his fellow occupants of Longwood, whom he roped into the exercise, willingly or not. General Bonaparte could be seen for hours of each day. He would wear a sun hat, working in the garden and was even overheard singing. The perimeter around the house was extended, as the area covered by the garden grew.

There were more departures. Early in 1819 Albine struck up a fast friendship with the much younger lieutenant of the 20th Regiment of Foot, Basil Jackson, erstwhile overseer of repairs at Longwood House and recent companion of Gaspard Gourgaud. Tongues wagged and the closeness of the Englishman and the colourful Frenchwoman was remarked upon by the Russian Commissioner Count Aleksandr Balmain to Bertrand. Jackson had been seen leaving Albine's quarters late in the evening.

When Jackson next visited her, she insisted they walk in the grounds, in plain view of the house, out of earshot. In distressed tones she told him that Napoleon had insisted they could no longer meet. He had confronted her, alleging an affair and that Jackson was Lowe's spy, using her to spy on him.

Jackson protested innocence and devotion and their friendship continued, enjoyed with regular walks (when it was dry enough – Longwood experienced rain on most days). They would arrange to meet so that he need not call at the house. The following month, a tearful Albine told Basil that Napoleon had forbidden further contact.

They discussed what could be done. She decided to leave. To remain at Longwood in the unhappy jealous atmosphere prevailing in the house, unable to see him, would be intolerable.

Sabine wrote to Lowe explaining she was ill with liver problems, requesting that she be permitted to return to Europe, together with her children (Napoleon wished her husband to remain), so that she might seek treatment and healthier conditions. Dr Stokoe, who now attended to the Longwood party, examined Sabine. Lowe (considering her a complication) decided to agree to her departure with her children, including three-year old Hélène. They embarked in July, witnessed by a tearful Napoleon.

One week later, under orders from Lowe to follow and report, Basil Jackson left. They would meet in Brussels, where they continued their liaison for a time. Sabine had drawn the intelligent, observant Jackson from St Helena.

It was noticed that the Emperor's time in St Helena could be divided into two periods. The first, his introduction to the island, his visible participation in social activities and exercise, an active man in good health, occupied in dictating his extensive memoirs and other works and the second, a time of withdrawal and decline, with a burst of gardening.

On 26 December 1819 a British orderly officer recorded "I saw General Bonaparte this afternoon in one of his little gardens in his dressing-gown. They are doing nothing but transplanting trees. Even this day, though Sunday, they are moving peach trees with fruit on them. They have been moving young oaks in full leaf, and the trees probably will survive, but the leaf is falling off as in Autumn."

After his long withdrawal into his rooms at Longwood, the emergence of the prisoner into plain view was a source of relief. There continued to be rumours and reports of escape and rescue plots, even false sightings as far away as America.

The previously robust health of General Bonaparte was in decline. He took less exercise and spent more time indoors. In February 1821 his condition deteriorated and he soon became an invalid. A known atheist, the patient, as he had become, was reconciled with the Catholic Church.

On the 5th of May 1821, having confessed, received Extreme Unction and after Viaticum, administered by Father Ange Vignalli (*Vinyally*), General Bonaparte died. His last reported words were "France, l'armee, tete d'armee, Josephine".

Days later the news reached Europe. Napoleon Bonaparte, the Corsican youth who had turned the World on its head and crowned himself Emperor of France, Master of Europe, had died in that far away, hard to imagine, lonely and windswept place. Some celebrated, many wept.

After various examinations, which concluded death was due to natural causes (stomach cancer[x]), and contrary to the Emperor's wishes, Sir Hudson Lowe (presumably acting on the orders of London, agreed with its Allies, not wanting the problems associated with a funeral in Britain or in France) arranged a simple burial on St Helena, in the Valley of the Willows. There were rumours of poisoning.

de Montholon served his master to the end.

The British, especially Sir Hudson Lowe, and the other Allied representatives would make no fuss. Death closed the matter very satisfactorily. St Helena lost its over-large garrison. The Royal Navy re-deployed its ships and the Allied Commissioners could return to their grateful masters.

The long-suffering Bertrands were free to leave. He was at this time under a death sentence should he return to France (he was later pardoned by Louis XVIII).

Marchand too could return, the chosen executor of the Emperor's last Testament, bearer of those most personal artefacts that he had been charged with distributing according to Napoleon's express wishes. Marchand was ennobled, with the status and title of a count, left 400,000 francs, with the words "the services he has rendered me are those of a friend." He was instructed to wed the daughter of an officer of the Old Imperial Guard[xi].

There would be stories, rumours and opinions as to the Great Man's demise – forests would be turned into print – did he die of natural causes or was he murdered? Who could be believed? Some cannot accept a prosaic end for their hero. The great strategist himself understood.

At the Palazzo D'Aste-Bonaparte in Rome, living with her brother, Cardinal Joseph Fesch, a mother visibly mourned. Madame Mère had shared in her son's first exile on Elba, suffered from his distant banishment.

PART II - THE EAGLET - "not a prisoner, but in a very special position"[xii]

On 22 July 1821, at Schonbrunn Palace, on the outskirts of Vienna, in his apartment on the third floor, with fine views overlooking the Kahlenberg, in the early evening a ten year-old boy was informed by his tutor, Jean de Foresti (deputed this sad task), that his father, whom he had barely known, but whom he loved and revered, was dead. Foresti wrote to Neipperg that "I saw more tears flow than I would have expected from a child who did not see or know his father".

Francis, advised by Metternich, determined that the Court would not mourn, only the boy was permitted this.

In Parma three months of official mourning were observed by Louise and her household. She wrote to her son "I have learned, my dear, that you have been very much moved by the misfortune which strikes us both, and it is for my heart, I feel, the best consolation, to write to you on this subject and to talk to you about it. I'm sure you felt a pain as deep as mine; for you would be an ingrate if you forgot all the goodness he had for you during your young years. You will strive to imitate his virtues, while avoiding the pitfalls he encountered."

There is no recorded reply and it was noticed that for quite some time after the boy did not speak of his father.

This boy, known within his mother's family circle as Franz, was being brought up in the stiffly formal environment of the Austrian Imperial Court. Already his short life had seen significant adjustments. Born the son and heir of an emperor, grandson of another, as King of Rome he succeeded his father briefly as Emperor Napoleon II after his abdication in 1814. Taken to Vienna after his mother returned, his grandfather and mother ignored his father's requests for the return of his wife and son after his return from Elba. Defeat at Waterloo lost his inheritance. He was stripped of all titles and rights to inherit from his father. In the eyes of his grandfather, by breaking his bonds in leaving Elba and once again threatening peace in Europe, the father became an outlaw.

Nevertheless, the boy was the son of his eldest daughter, his own flesh and blood. For a Habsburg, family and the position and security of the family came first. Francis was not vengeful toward this innocent. His determination, in consultation with Klemens Metternich (*Metterrnih*), his chief counsellor, was that the boy should be brought up at court under close supervision and in the manner of a Habsburg prince.

Louise was joyful at her husband's defeat at Waterloo, confirmation of her freedom to remain under her father's aegis, to pursue her relationship with von Neipperg, her relationship of choice, her duty done. She wrote "Dear Father, I hope that we will have a lasting peace now since the Emperor Napoleon will never trouble it again. I hope he will be treated with kindness and clemency, and I beg you, dear father, to contribute to it. This is the sole prayer I can dare to pray for, and this is the last time I will deal with his fate; I thank him for the quiet indifference in which he let me live instead of making me unhappy."

His mother's attitude towards Franz's upbringing was explained in a letter to Mme. de Montebello "I want him raised in the principles of my country, and I will explain it to you. I want to make quite a German prince so loyal, so brave, I want, when he grows up, that he serve his new homeland. It will be his talents, his spirit, his chivalry that will make him a name, because the one he has from birth is unfortunately not beautiful."

Napoleon (and Bonapartists generally) would have been apoplectic to read this confirmation of his worst fears for his son's future. Two contrasting and opposed forces of love and nurture, indoctrination, irreconcilable destinies.

Louise was in step with her father. She had paid the price for dynastic survival. On one issue they diverged; Francis and Metternich were set that the prince should not leave Vienna. When Louise, now styled Duchess of Parma, sought to take her young son there, Francis ordered that the boy could not accompany her.

He was nervous of the consequences of Napoleon's son arriving in Italy and needed to assure his Allies, especially England, that Parma would not end up in the hands of this boy. A secret pact was made between Austria, Russia and Prussia to adjust the Treaty of Paris of 1814, under which Franz would succeed his mother.

Francis made arrangements for his grandson's education. The Prince's circle was forbidden to mention or discuss his past with him. Francis wrote "it is necessary to dismiss everything that can remind him of the existence he has led so far." He was to be raised a German.

The Emperor selected Count Maurice Dietrichstein (*Dyetrihstein*), a reliable guardian of the interests of the Habsburg House[xiii], to oversee Franz's upbringing. Dietrichstein drew up a programme of education and appointed tutors. Francis remained in close touch.

Napoleon had sought to surround his son with a small group of trusted French carers. People he could rely upon to remind the son of his father, of his destiny.

This group comprised Claude Meneval, Mme. de Montesquiou, Mme. Marchand (mother of Napoleon's valet, with him on St Helena) and Mme. Soufflot, her daughter. One by one they were sent away. The last to leave was Mme. Marchand, for sending a lock of the boy's hair to St Helena in response to a request that reached her from her son.

Pressed by Louise to outline a future for her son, Francis responded. In 1817 a treaty confirmed that on his mother's death Parma would pass not to him, but to the Duchess of Lucca. He granted properties in Bohemia to young Franz, generating some 500,000 francs per year. He was patented as Duke of Reichstadt, his arms, rank and income awarded by Francis, no mention of his father.

Louise lost no time in tying the marital knot once she was free. She was expecting Neipperg's child. Mourning over, they married, on 8 August 1821, in a quiet ceremony presided over by Father Giovanni Tommaso Neuschel[xiv].

She had already borne Neipperg two children, Alberta (in May 1817) and Guillaume Alberto in (1819). Treason in the eyes of Bonapartists. Franz felt affection for von Neipperg.

Franz was Napoleon's only legitimate heir. Heir to a great fortune. Before Napoleon departed from Paris in 1815 he had deposited almost 6 million United States Dollars[xv] with Lafitte, the banker, against a double receipt. Napoleon's last Will and Testament charged Lafitte, Montholon, Bertrand and Marchand with its distribution.

Austria and France were angry with Britain for permitting the Will to be made public. This presaged infighting. Lafitte refused to accept his fellow executors and would not release the funds. Neipperg, encouraged by Louise, pressed Metternich to intervene on Franz's behalf and Louise nominated Count Dietrichstein her attorney to act for her son's interests. Metternich considered whether to mount a challenge for half of the property of the boy's father?

Napoleon had not designated these funds for his son. Instead, he designated for him to receive his most personal items - his Austerlitz epée, his camp beds, spyglass, watches, guns, silverware, library, necklace of the Legion d'Honneur and sword as First Consul. His most valued personal treasures, they did not reach Franz.

A total of 9 million United States Dollars was the official sum of Napoleon's legacy. Lafitte returned only 3.5 million Dollars out of the funds deposited with him. Substantial sums were paid to the French Treasury.[xvi]

Once Louise and he obtained a copy of Napoleon's Will, Neipperg challenged the British Government to explain why it did not disclose those funds Napoleon was believed to have deposited with Baring Brothers, the London bankers, for safekeeping?[xvii]

Austria pressed Paris to recover some of these monies, but the Will was valid and the Duke of Reichstadt (and the Bonaparte family as a whole) had been dispossessed of all civil and property rights in France under a law passed in 1816.

Franz was a gifted student of military matters, mathematics, German and Italian and was taught chemistry, physics and biology. Contrary to rumours, he was not forbidden to learn French, the lingua franca of diplomatic Europe and the elite. He was taught to play the piano (not well) under the direction of a M. Eybler.

Francis, sensitive to accusations of neglecting his grandson's education, established commissions of academics, the court prelate, senior army officers and other advisers to oversee his education and training.

Franz was brought up in solitude, educated alone, often without other children to play with and then they were his Habsburg cousins. His mother was often away in Parma. He was treated as a member of the Imperial family and the Emperor was fond of him. He liked his comfortable, if chilly at times, rooms on the third floor at Schonbrunn Palace, with their fine views of the square in front of the Palace and of the Kahlenberg, reaching to Dornbach. A coterie of 20 - 30 persons were responsible for his welfare, development and security.

As the boy became a teenager, he became a focus of interest by those who saw in him a successor to his father, who could once again unite them and lead them back towards the glory, independence or other bright future they associated with him, hopes extinguished or suppressed along with his flame.

There were various attempts to reach out to him, gain his attention, to gauge his awareness and interest.

Paris, Berlin and Moscow were determined to ensure that the Prince was incubated from infection by these causes, neutered. Francis and Metternich shared these concerns. They had no wish to see the balance of power upset once more. They were well aware of the building pressures of nationalist and anarchist causes. The Prince was guarded and watched.

When from France came news of a plot kill to King
Louis, to restore Napoleon II, the French ambassador, M.
de Caraman reported "I am assured every day that the
subordinates around the Duke of Reichstadt have been
put there by the police and report directly to the
administration. Count Sedlinstky, head of the department,
applies a religious conscience to it. The Emperor charged
him with the selection of these individuals and he is
responsible for anything that occurs in the inner circle of
the young Duke. The Count has assured me that everyone
surrounding the Duke has been placed there by him and is
answerable to him." [xviii]

Cries of "Long live the Emperor! Long live the King of
Rome!" were heard in France. There were uprisings,
mainly led by former junior Bonapartist army officers,
but all failed or were suppressed. They were organised or
supported well enough to carry realistic prospects of
success. It was a romantic notion, a tragedy for those few
who gave their lives or liberty.

In late November 1823 Signor Petrucci, after an
increasingly anxious wait of 90 days, prepared to do as he
had been instructed. Should his partner not have returned
or contacted him he must travel to Paris to deliver a
sealed letter into the hand of Louis ("only the King
himself").

On 23 August 1823 the comfortably private way of life of
Signor Revard was interrupted by a visitor with an urgent
message. He packed a valise and left.

Revard travelled by coach to Vienna with the good-humoured ripostes of a doppelgänger, jokes of escape from St Helena. When pressed, he would say that he found life safer now that his twin was dead.

He went to an address in Hietzing, in the vicinity of Schonbrunn Palace, arriving in darkness.

Schulmeister's agents, recruited when he was Chief of Police in Vienna, briefed him on the location of his son's apartment in the familiar palace nearby, preparations were made.

Armed Guards patrolled at all times, but the grounds were extensive, wooded around the perimeter, affording cover on a cloudy night. A member of the household would meet him on the other side. They would take passages used only by servants and the amorous. Servants, those not asleep, tired at the end of their day's labour, coming across strangers in these dark corridors knew better than to be inquisitive, though it was interesting to see whose rooms were entered.

Revard was excited and anxious. Nine years had passed since he last saw, held his beautiful little boy. He had longed for him and fretted over his captivity in the hands of his enemies these long years. Excitement was tempered by his worries for the boy's health. His life was at risk, was the report from a reliable source.

Concerns as to how the boy would react on meeting his father, appearing in his rooms, raised from the dead.

Discovery, capture and all that might follow. Incalculable consequences. Francis and Metternich might simply murder him and bury the evidence.

See his boy again, he must; it was a compulsion and his new life in Verona, while a comfortable but dull existence, was only that. He had faced danger and death so many times. It would be better than dying in bed.

It was a long day of waiting.

That night, 4 September 1823, in the early hours, a patrolling sentry, used to the mindless task of patrolling his designated beat inside the perimeter walls, the night sounds of nature, was astonished to see a ladder, the dark silhouette of a man dressed in a dark cloak dimly lit by moonlight outlined in contrast against the whitewashed stucco wall. He shouted his challenge to halt or be shot. The intruder responded by climbing faster. He fired and did not miss. With a yell, the figure fell. He approached the still, warm body. Whistles and shouts of the rapidly approaching. Commotion.

His mind reeled when he saw the face of his kill.

More Guards and others from the household arrived hot foot.

The officer of the watch had the presence of mind to cover the body, to place Guards in a perimeter. Louise and von Neipperg, staying at the Palace, were called to the scene, where he took charge. All but a handful of the Guards on the scene were sent away, ordered to silence.

There was an intruder, possibly a misguided assassin or thief. He was dead and the police would take over. After the excitement they went back to bed.

A second ladder was found on the outside of the perimeter wall, the footprints of more than one person. A large police presence could only excite interest.

The covered body was stretchered into a cellar in the Palace. No-one was permitted access.

The French Ambassador was summoned and, to his astonishment, informed. He readily agreed to preserving the utmost secrecy - if news got out that Napoleon had escaped St Helena, lived as a free man until now and had been shot by the Austrians as if he were a common thief or assassin it could have incalculable consequences. It was inconceivable!

An unmarked grave was dug in the Palace grounds and into this hole was laid to rest the erstwhile conqueror of Europe and Emperor of France.

Another conspiracy was born; the conspiracy of silence of those who knew this explosive secret.

As the news reached them, those few most trusted family-members and former subordinates who had maintained their devotion to her son and his cause, and been aware of his secret existence, also felt the true loss of a loved one, a powerful life force finally and truly extinguished. Madame Mère wept real tears.

Franz was now not only the publicly acknowledged heir to his father; he was so in their eyes too. Long live the King of Rome! Long live Napoleon II!

In December 1823, having insisted that he see the King himself, with the message that he had in his possession a letter to the King from Napoleon Bonaparte, Signor Petrucci was eventually permitted to fulfil his commission. The letter was placed into the King's hand - the hand of a man who had heard an extraordinary tale from Vienna. Signor Petrucci knew the true identity of his former partner.[xix] He returned to Verona, where the illusion was maintained. His partner had left. Petrucci was suddenly a wealthy man, but what could you expect of a diamond merchant?

By the age of 17, in 1828, Franz was six-foot tall, unusual for the time, a young adult and a very promising soldier – too promising. It was his chosen career. His progress was a matter of developing concern, especially in France, where social unrest provided fertile ground for political interference and memories of the boy's father and his glory days were recent. Bonapartists were influential, with eyes and hopes turning towards the maturing young challenger.

Metternich received regular reports (police updates, compiled from informants, and reports from Count Dietrichstein) on the young Bonaparte, monitoring his development, activities and inclinations and keeping a record of with whom he met and who made up his circle.

This young man was to be kept on a short rein, forbidden any political activism, out of reach of those who would encourage him to ambitions of pursuing his father's legacy. He was nevertheless a useful piece on the chessboard in Austria's relations with its neighbour France.

As Franz grew up he was increasingly determined to be his own man. From an early age the prince would question his entourage and Francis himself about his father and about his own former title as King of Rome. He insisted on having and regularly studying a copy of 'Les Fastes de la France', an historical work in which were described details of his father's victories.

Metternich and Francis began to observe the young man's growing frustration with the tight reins on which he was being controlled and the denial of his French, Corsican, family and imperial heritages. Francis ordered that the boy's questions should be answered openly and truthfully.

Franz found solace in studying military matters, developing his career in the Army and in a burgeoning friendship.

Antoine von Prokesch-Osten was 16 years his senior, the son of a provincial administrator in Gratz, Styria. He was not born a noble, but this able man, as a young law student, fought against France in 1813-14 for German liberation, again in 1815 as an ordnance officer under Archduke Charles, subsequently teaching mathematics at the Olmutz Cadet School, where he came to the attention of Prince Schwartzenburg. His climb was rapid.

It was the publication of his written piece on the Battle of Waterloo, complimenting Napoleon's generalship, which appeared in the Österreichische Militärzeitschrift in 1819, that first caught Franz's attention.

They met in 1830 in Gratz, when the Emperor's court came to visit the town. Prokesch was invited to dine at the Imperial table and placed next to Franz.

On the following day Prokesch was summoned by Dietrichstein to meet the Duke of Reichstadt. Eagerly the Prince approached him with greetings "You have known me and I have loved you for a long time. You have defended the honour of my father at a time when everyone slandered him at will. I read your memoir on the Battle of Waterloo, and to better penetrate each line, I translated it twice, first in French, then in Italian".

Prokesch recorded "I answered in words inspired by the desire to bind myself closely with this handsome young man, so deluded in this world".[xx]

No one was allowed by Dietrichstein to have access to the Prince who was not vetted and sanctioned by Francis, in consultation with Metternich. The Neipperg stratagem had succeeded spectacularly with the lonely mother (recently widowed and very sad over Neipperg's passing). It succeeded again with the lonely son.

The publication to the whole Army of an article unfashionably praising the boy's father was rich bait.

Dietrichstein introduced the topic of Greece, where a ten-year war of independence had been fought against Ottoman rule, with interventions by the British, the Russians and the French. On the previous day, following dinner, Prokesch ventured "In the presence of the Archduke John, Count Maurice [Dietrichstein], [and] Colonel Werklein, Steward of the Archduchess Marie Louise, I had, taking advantage of a moment when the Duke of Reichstadt was occupied elsewhere, slipped into the conversation the idea that the throne of Greece, lacking pretenders since the refusal of the Prince of Coburg, could not be given to a more worthy than the son of Napoleon. This proposal had, to my great surprise, received general approval. The Imperatrice [Caroline] herself who, during this conversation, had approached us, did not seem opposed to it... Now, Count Maurice [Dietrichstein] having provided me with the same morning once more the opportunity to speak of Greece, the Duke would soon guess my thoughts and catch fire at my words."

Their conversation was interrupted by a young female visitor. The Duke excused himself for a few minutes. When he returned, he impressed upon Prokesch and Dietrichstein that rather than a Greek adventure he wanted to become a soldier, to follow in his father's footsteps, to become a great general, a commander of armies. A commander who wished it to be clearly understood that he did not want to be or be seen to be a threat to Europe or to act contrary to the interests of France or Austria, of his French family or his Austrian family, most particularly his grandfather.

Their enthusiastic discussion of his father's military manoeuvres and strategy, convinced Prokesch of the capabilities of this young man. They were interrupted again by the same young lady with a summons to Prokesch to attend upon Archduchess Louise. They went to her together.

Prokesch wrote that the boy unburdened himself to him "my heart is far from being ungrateful to Austria; but it seems to me that, once seated on the throne of France, I could lend my country a more effective support than by confining myself to following in the footsteps of Prince Eugene[xxi]. If I opted for this last role, it is in order to commence the career of arms, the only one that suits the son of Napoleon. And if ever I come to acquire the slightest military glory, it will be one more step towards the throne. I cannot be an adventurer, nor do I want to become a toy. The situation must clear in France before I consent to set foot there. For the moment, my task is to make myself able to command an army. I will not negotiate anything that can lead to this goal. We do not learn war in books, they say; but is not every strategic conception a model for awakening ideas? Does not getting familiar with historical narratives establish real and living relationships, not only with writers, but with the very actors of the great drama of history?"

The Prince pointed to a newspaper that lay on his desk, at an article reporting on events in Poland, "if the general war comes to burst, if the prospect of reigning in France vanishes for me, if we are called to see the unity of Poland arise from the heart of this cataclysm, I would like her to call me, and it is time to repair one of the greatest iniquities of the past."[xxii] [xxiii]

We may be confident that Prokesch reported this conversation. The Prince was nineteen years old - a young man, beginning to know his own mind, to seek his path and destiny, one that would reflect well in the shadow of his great father, very aware of the responsibility attaching to his name and legacy. His grandfather, Metternich and others, who included the leaders of France, Russia, Prussia and Britain, were watching carefully. He must not be allowed to become a problem.

In the febrile atmosphere of 1830 the Prince was a piece on the chess board.

Metternich was becoming convinced that Franz could not be relied upon to do as bidden, especially once he held reins of power: "at the end of six months the Duke of Reichstadt would be surrounded by ambitions, demands, resentments, hatreds and conspiracies; he would be on the edge of the abyss…the Emperor [Francis] is too fond of his principles and his duties toward his people, as well as the happiness of his grandson, to ever lend himself to such proposals". He also wrote 'to make Bonapartism without Bonaparte is an absolutely false idea. When with his genius, which will not be found easily, Napoleon managed to tame and subjugate the French Revolution, he needed a set of circumstances that favoured his projects" and, finally, "greatness seldom passes from father to son".[xxiv]

The death of Louis XVIII in 1824 prompted a crisis. Charles X made an unpopular monarchy even more so by his attempts to reassert the ancien regime, to roll back the changes for which so much blood of his compatriots had been shed. In July 1830 it produced a revolution.

Charles' abdication (and flight to Britain[xxv]) could have been an opportunity for the reinstatement of Napoleon II, as some Bonapartists hoped, but there was no prospect of his grandfather permitting this and no realistic chance of exfiltrating the Prince to set him on the throne.

Into this opportunity stepped Louis-Philippe, from the Orleans branch of the Bourbon family, supported by a mixture of the government in London, English bankers, the wealthy bourgeoisie and some former Bonapartist army officers.

Meanwhile, the Bonaparte Family were keenly aware of their lack of contact with the scion of their House. This presented many practical problems. One of which was to even assess the young man's orientation and capabilities. What could they hope for from him? How could they reach out to him? Who could be relied upon?

Another Bonaparte was chosen. Napoleone, daughter of Elisa Bonaparte, Grand Duchess of Tuscany, and Felix Bacciochi. Napoleone was married to a man rather older than her, Count Philippe Camerata Passionei of Mazzolino. She was a game girl who enjoyed horse riding, hunting and fencing.

Franz, growing up fast and seeking his destiny, was politely, but firmly, pressing his grandfather and Metternich, whom he sought to reassure. In September 1830 he told Metternich "the essential object of my life is not to remain unworthy of the glory of my father: I think I can achieve this high goal if, as much as I can, I manage one day to appropriate some of his high qualities, striving to avoid the pitfalls that befell him. I would fail in the duties his memory imposes on me if I became the toy of factions and the instrument of intrigues. The son of Napoleon can never descend to the despicable role of an adventurer".

Unrest in France was followed by a riot in Belgium, which proclaimed its independence from France. The possibility of the Duke becoming its king was mooted but not encouraged in Vienna.

In October 1830 the Countess Camerata travelled to Vienna alone, staying there in an hotel. She hoped to approach her cousin in the Prater Park, where it had become his custom to walk. The Prince was rarely seen in public and was always escorted. Napoleone soon realised that she could not go up to the Prince and speak with him alone.

She made the acquaintance of Baron Oberhaus, a member of the Prince's entourage, who invited her to his home to a gathering.

Franz was excited to meet his cousin, this lively young woman who so obviously wanted to speak with him. He felt keenly the starvation of news from his father's family. When she suggested they meet alone in a corridor, leaving the room separately, he was happy to oblige, intrigued.

Baron Oberhaus was no fool. He followed them. When he challenged the Countess "what are you doing, Madame?", Napoleone retorted "who will refuse me to kiss the hand of the son of my sovereign?" and did so.

Napoleone knew that she was watched and not trusted. She would not have another opportunity to speak with the Prince, certainly not alone. She resorted to bribing a servant of Oberhaus' to deliver a letter to her cousin. It was passed to Oberhaus, to Dietrichstein and thence to Prokesch, who showed it to the Prince. According to Prokesch, Napoleone wrote

"Vienna, November 17, 1830

Prince, I write to you for the third time. Please let me know by word if you have received my letters and if you want to act as an Austrian archduke or a French prince. In the first case, hand over my letters. In giving me up, you will probably gain a higher position, and this act of devotion will be attributed to you. But if, on the contrary, you wish to profit by my advice, if you act like a man, then, prince, you will see how much obstacles yield to a calm and strong will. You will find a thousand means to speak to me, that alone I cannot embrace. You can only believe in yourself. Put out of your mind any idea of entrusting yourself to someone else. Know that if I asked to see you, even in front of a hundred witnesses, my request would be refused, that you are dead for all that is

French or of your family. In the name of the horrible torments to which the kings of Europe have condemned your father, thinking of this agony of the banished, by which they made him expiate the crime of having been too generous to them, remember that you are his son, that the sight of him in death rested on your image, [let it] penetrate you with so much horror, and inflict on them no other punishment than that of seeing you seated on the throne of France. Profit from this moment, prince. I may have said too much: my fate is in your hands, and I can tell you that if you use my letters for my downfall, the idea of your cowardice will make me suffer more than anything else they can do to me. The man who will give you this letter will take care of your answer. If you have honor, you will not refuse me.

Napoleone C. Camerata "

Prokesch was sent to warn the Countess to leave Vienna and not return. He told her that he came on the Prince's behalf. He wanted her to leave, to cease any activities that could embarrass him and even affect his liberty.

Prokesch questioned her about the Bonapartist party. Who had put her up to this, he demanded to know? Napoleone said she was acting alone. She was bundled out of Vienna.

Questioned by the police, her husband claimed he had no knowledge of the affair. His wife was a strong-willed independent woman.

The November Uprising in Poland proclaimed a provisional government under the brief presidency of a former Napoleonic general, a veteran of the Russian campaign of 1812 and other actions, General Józef Chłopicki (*Hwopitski*).[xxvi]

Franz was aware of these events, widely discussed at Court and in the newspapers. His brief contact with Napoleone Bonaparte, had at least assured him of the ongoing interest of his father's family. That he could not expect his grandfather or Metternich to allow him to become embroiled in these events was made clear to him.

The realpolitik of the fragile economic state of Austria-Hungary, its dependency upon London bankers and not upsetting Whitehall, the growing military ascendancy of its Russian and Prussian neighbours all stood in the way.

He understood their position, but it was not his position, it was his circumstance and he did nothing to be seen to encourage these factions.

In January 1831 Francis concluded it would be safe to permit his grandson greater latitude to go out into society. This would cheer the boy up, distract him from his lonely brooding existence, fixated on his father, his future and military matters and would go some way to answering accusations that he had imprisoned his own grandson.

By this time things were looking more promising, from Francis's perspective, in France and in Poland, where grip was being applied. It seemed unlikely that the boy could get into trouble and, in any event, he would remain on a leash, just a slightly longer one. If he enjoyed himself too much that would be helpful.

Franz attended a ball held by the British Ambassador, Lord Cowley, on 25 January 1831. The Prince took to social life with gusto, attending salons, becoming a regular at the theatre.

He was well aware that he was under constant surveillance. Very little surprised his grandfather. In many respects this was for his own protection. He was a split personage, heir to Napoleon and Habsburg prince, opposing weights on his conscience, loyalties and love.

The focus of the reports being received by Metternich and the Emperor was increasingly on the handsome young Duke's growing interest in and effect upon the ladies. They hoped for some suitably compliant girl of good enough family, or even just a discreet maid or two. It was in part what the secret police were there to deal with, protecting the Imperial Family, even from itself if need be. No other dynasty in Europe had advanced and protected itself so effectively for so long. Scandal had to be avoided, contained if not anticipated, and dealt with.[xxvii]

Prokesch sought to procure a relationship for the Prince with a singer, a Miss Peche. Franz declined.

Count Esterhazy wanted to arrange an affair with Countess Naudine Caroly but, according to Prokesch, this also came to nothing, "nature was awakening in this young man of twenty. He often spoke to me of his impressions with the tone of the purest innocence. Never would he have so expressed himself with such frankness if he had had more intimate relations with the fair sex - he would have betrayed himself by his embarrassment".

Two Viennese sisters, Therese and Fanny Elssler, on the heels of successes in Naples and Berlin, captivated Viennese audiences with their balletic skill and beauty, most especially the younger, Fanny, beginning a long and successful international career. Her most famous character dance would become the Spanish La Cachucha ("The Cap").

A voluptuous brunette with a perfect complexion, Fanny inspired passions wherever she went. At 16, performing in Naples, she caught the eye of the elderly heir to the throne of the Two Sicilies, Leopold, Prince of Salerno, brother to the King and married to a Habsburg Archduchess. Leopold, a ruthless man, was determined to have her. He pressed his case on her mother with offers of money so insistently that in fear of what he might do she assented. It was said that Leopold was "Fanny's first purchaser, who had her body without touching her soul!"[xxviii]

The news reached Vienna and Leopold was instructed to present himself in Rome, newly appointed to the Papal Guard of Honour.

Fanny returned to Vienna where she bore Leopold a son, Franz Robert Elssler, brought up by her relatives.

On 25 November 1829 she had put in her first performance in the leading role in 'The Fairy and the Knight', an acclaimed performance. In the audience was

Friedrich von Gentz, more than three times her age, famed political writer, Imperial Counsellor, friend and adviser of Metternich. On 5 December he watched again as Fanny performed as Emma in Horschelt's 'Der Berggeist' (The Mountain Spirit) - it turned his head. He arranged for four lovely camelias to be delivered to the theatre for Fanny, with his card. He contrived a meeting - on 4 January 1830 they coincided at a musical soiree arranged by Countess Gallenberg. More visits to the theatre followed and more gifts too. By the Spring, aided and abetted by Count Robert von Gallenberg (Director of the Vienna Opera), Gentz was a regular visitor to the Elsslers' home.

That Summer their relationship, between a foolish smitten old man enjoying a totally unexpected last flourish of romantic ardour and a young, beautiful and increasingly famous woman, saw them together each day.

Fanny's reputation was spreading. Contracted to appear in October and November 1830 in Berlin, Fanny was a great success. Meanwhile Gentz pined for her, supported by friends such as Prokesch. She returned in December.

Over the following months their relationship became one of warm friendship. Gentz was feeling and showing his advancing years. Another invitation to perform in Berlin in mid 1831, a contract for Fanny and her sister, brought with it looming separation, felt keenly by Gentz, who wrote "even now my heart bleeds at the thought of this parting, and I really do not know how I shall bear it this time."[xxix]

Gentz took to bringing Prokesch on evening visits to Fanny's apartment in Karntnerstrasse, Hietzing, close to Schonbrunn Palace. Prokesch wrote 'we had a room there called 'Portici', reserved for our communal readings and our work, pleasantly furnished and full of flowers, the most delightful place imaginable. Between ten and eleven o'clock Fanny brought us coffee, and with full confidence in one another we read or talked among ourselves." Gentz and Prokesch continued their visits to Portici even after Fanny and her sister had again departed for Berlin on 14 November 1831. This time Fanny would be away for three months.

In Berlin Fanny appeared in a succession of acclaimed productions, including 'La Fille mal gardée', a comedy, co-produced with Anton Stuhlmuller, her dancing partner, also Viennese. Metternich was concerned his old friend was making something of a fool of himself.

By mid-February 1832 Metternich was receiving intelligence reports from Berlin of developing intimacy between Fanny and Stuhlmuller. There were also reports of a dalliance with the King of Prussia, who had shown obvious interest and showered her with expensive gifts. Metternich warned Prokesch. These revelations would devastate Gentz, increasingly fragile and emotional.

Fanny was soon back in Vienna. Attentive to him, her balletic performances continuing, Gentz fading. Metternich saw Fanny as an opportunist.

Franz was living close to the Hietzing apartment and was, since his grandfather permitted him to go out in public, a regular in the audience, obvious that he found Fanny fascinating. Prokesch and Gentz introduced them. Gossip spread.

Helen Grote wrote that Fanny told her "Gentz was terrified at any indication of Fanny's preference for anyone else. In particular he was desperately jealous of the young Duke of Reichstadt...whose admiration for the charming danseuse was publicly known, and to no one more unmistakably than to Fanny herself. Never was His Royal Highness known to miss a ballet wherein she appeared, and his earnest gaze was always directed to her movements during the evening. Fanny used to peep through the slit in the drop curtain before the performance began, and would exclaim "Ah, voila mon petit Prince! toujours a son poste!" He was constantly to be seen walking on the fortifications near to which the Elssler family lived in the hope of seeing Fanny as she went to the theatre... I have more than once questioned Fanny on this point, and her replies convinced me that she had been effectively prevented from encouraging the passion of her royal admirer. Her mother exercised a watchful control over her daughters, never leaving them unattended when out of the house, and when in it, little danger was to be apprehended. They occupied a flat some three stories up with a single door of entry so that no one could come in unobserved."

Mrs Grote related that she had asked Fanny "So you never really had the curiosity to make the Prince's acquaintance?" to which Fanny replied to her "I should have liked to do so, but I was so closely guarded that it was difficult. My mother trembled as to what might befall her, if the higher powers suspected that the Duke had formed an acquaintance with me, and accordingly I dared not so much as look out of the window. I might perhaps have liked to have a Napoleon as a lover, but it would have been the death of Gentz. I knew that. I could not bear to cause his death. He was after a manner too dear to me." Fanny and her family were well aware of their situation.[xxx]

Rumours of an affair with the Duke persisted. The Prince and the Showgirl, two young, beautiful and interesting people, in the public eye - a hackneyed cliché that sold theatre tickets.

At Lord Cowley's ball Franz was excited to meet one of his father's marshals, Auguste de Marmont, Duke of Ragusa[xxxi] (whom many, including Napoleon, regarded as a traitor, for his secretly negotiated surrender in 1814, precipitating the end). Marmont recorded "my eyes went eagerly on him. I saw him for the first time from near and with ease. I found in him the look of his father...."

The Prince invited the Marshal to visit to discuss his father's campaigns and, with Metternich's permission, Marmont did.

Marmont wrote the Prince impressed upon him "if the policy of the sovereigns of Europe determined them to put me forward, I would solemnly protest. The son of Napoleon must be too great to serve as an instrument, and in events of this nature, I do not want to be a vanguard but a reserve, that is to … arrive as a help in recalling great memories."

It was a prudent message to Marmont, who could be relied upon to relay it. Franz had hopes he might yet have a role, but he could not trust a man who had betrayed his father.

Three weeks later Franz's patience was tested too far. Distressing news reached him that the rebellion in Modena, that had spread within the Romagna, had extended to Parma, where a popular uprising resulted in his mother being imprisoned in her own palace.

Franz went quickly to his grandfather to urge him to send him with his regiment to his mother's aid. This was something he could do, his duty, and it could not conflict with the interests of his grandfather and even Metternich, surely?

Franz knew only so much. Metternich had received reports from his agents in Italy. The insurgency was encouraged by another Habsburg kinsman, the Duke of Modena, Francis IV of Habsburg-Este, ambitious to increase his domain. Learning he had been rumbled and seeking to recover from his gambit, the Duke of Modena had done an about-face and arrested the ringleader, but the revolt continued and spread. Its objective was to establish a kingdom of Italy, taking lands from the Pope, as a constitutional monarchy - with Franz as king!

Francis refused his grandson permission to aid his mother. Italy was a powder keg and his grandson's arrival could set it off. Anything could happen.

Franz wrote "I am rather unhappy, here I am obliged to lose the first opportunity that was presented to me to show my mother all my devotion to her. I was so sweet to help her and in such circumstances I am reduced to offering sterile consolations, this is the first time I have been in pain to obey the orders of the Emperor." He did not write "my grandfather".

Franz's realisation was crushing. He was to live out a pointless existence. His grandfather had so resolved. It was the breaking point. He was watched too closely for this not to be anticipated, but not closely enough.

For much of 1831 Anton von Prokesch was in Italy, sent by Metternich, who appointed him Chief of Staff of the Austrian Army of Italy. He said goodbye to the Prince on 31 March, before departing for Bologna, to be active in the campaign that Franz had dearly wished to participate in.

He was ordered to return to Vienna in early October, residing in Hietzing. He recorded "I thought the Duke looked good enough, though a little thin, and my impression was that he was being fatigued with too much care. What he needed was movement, material activity, to stifle the fire that devoured his soul. He seemed decidedly calmer. His desires had remained the same, but his hopes had diminished. during the long interval in which we had remained distant from each other, he had not perceived on the political horizon any sign which presaged that in France his wish was seriously desired; in Poland the insurrection was no more than an ordinary sedition on the eve of being repressed; in Italy secret societies alone were still agitated, and this country offered no arena worthy of the name. This name, which he regarded as a sacred inheritance, he saw to profane in many places by the Revolution. I myself did not have any further information, except that I knew that the members of the Bonaparte family, with no purpose other than to stir up trouble, took part in the impotent riots that took place in Italy, and that the party which, in France, was trying to overthrow [Louis-Philippe], was the republican faction and not the Napoleonic party. I had to suppose...that if the last of these parties existed more or less widespread in the country, it was there in a state of complete impotence. I was not unaware that openings had been made in Vienna, or that they had been rejected."

Dietrichstein intercepted a passionate letter "from a lady of the court, a Pole and a canoness[xxxii], also very pretty, intended for Franz "hero of romance", "eagle raised in a henhouse"".[xxxiii] [xxxiv]

This missive was not the beginning or the limit of the correspondence between Franz and Melanie, the 18-year-old daughter of Graf Samuel Kostrowicki ("*Kostrovitzky*", phonetically spelt in German).

We do not know whether records of their secretive correspondence still exist, hidden in some dusty box or file in a locked away archive, perhaps, waiting to be revealed or not. We can imagine the excitement and private passion of a young man of 20 years and a girl of 18, both attractive, one the caged son of a foreign hero to her countrymen, a symbol of hope that they could regain their past independence, self-determination and even glory - a romantic notion shared by many compatriots, at home and in exile. Brought together by Fate in the gilded surroundings of the Imperial Court, they were innocents sharing an impossible love, risking discovery at any time.

It must have been a tour de force for Melanie and we may wonder at whether Franz, for a short time, found love, not in the arms of an actress or ballet dancer, but in those of a young, fresh, accomplished, beautiful and lively noblewoman, who was able to come and go to and from the Palace without, at least initially, gaining unwelcome suspicious attention?

Perhaps this relationship was the spark that gave rise to the Prince's interest in Poland, recorded by Anton Prokesch "if the general war comes to burst, if the prospect of reigning in France vanishes for me, if we are called to see the unity of Poland arise from the heart of this cataclysm, I would like her to call me, and it is time to repair one of the greatest iniquities of the past", a view surely instilled in her by Melanie's patriotic family?

Perhaps he did briefly entertain speculative thoughts. If so, these were desperate thoughts, as both his doomed relationship with Melanie and realpolitik would demonstrate.

In the late Autumn of 1831 Franz's health began to deteriorate. He developed a persistent cough and loss of weight and his appetite was poor. All noticeable in this tall and thin young man. Dietrichstein instructed the renowned Dr. Johann Malfatti[xxxv] to examine Franz. Malfatti lived conveniently nearby on Küniglberg, a hill in Hietzing.

The revelation to the Emperor and to Metternich, when it came, that despite surrounding Franz with persons responsible for safeguarding him he had conducted a liaison with this young Polish countess was shocking.

Did Louise, who had had matrimonial peccadilloes to resolve with the aid of the Catholic Church, in which she was assisted by Father Neuschel, her confessor, intercede? We do not know how the secret was revealed or who by - perhaps only once Melanie found herself pregnant, disclosing this to Franz and in confession to her parents? Was his grandfather informed by Franz or Louise, or by Metternich or another informer? Did Louise arrange a wedding, officiated in camera?

Meanwhile, Franz's widely noted fascination with Fanny Elssler still fed the gossips. Newssheets contained suggestions of a marriage between Franz and the daughter of Archduke Charles. Rumours circulated of him having a liaison at Court, of a secret wedding. A rumour circulated that Franz was unusually close to the Emperor's daughter-in-law, Frederique-Sophie, daughter of the King of Bavaria, married at 19 to a boorish husband, the Emperor's son Francois-Charles-Joseph.[xxxvi]

There was in motion an elaborate mechanism of wheels within wheels, one wheel turning, our attention taken by another, and on it went.

Louis Marchand, seeking to fulfil his late master's instructions and to deliver to Franz those precious items of his father's left to be given into his possession, applied to Metternich for permission to see Franz. He was refused, on medical grounds. Malfatti said this was to avoid provoking too much emotional strain on a young man made fragile by his illness.

Franz went into a decline. On 4 February 1832 he wrote to his mother "forgive me today for a trembling script, a short letter, but I am still very weak. I have been in bed for six days, and I am recovering for a week. The fever, vehement enough in truth, has completely stopped, but the chills, which harass me more than all the fatigues which I remember, return regularly each evening. However, I believe they will end one day. I am armed with a lot of patience, and I am looking for glory to suffer patiently."

He recovered sufficiently to hope that he might go to Naples, to visit Prokesch.

In April 1832.Franz insisted on watching a horse race and was soaked by rain. He returned to his rooms with a fever, his coughing persistent, soon spitting up blood and complaining of a sharp pain on the right side of his chest, day and night.

Princess Melanie von Metternich recorded 'the Emperor told Clement that he had met doctors in consultation to decide on the condition of the Duke of Reichstadt and that all had declared that the situation of the patient seemed desperate to them. He is already spitting out pieces of lung and has only a few months to live."

The ailing Gentz passed away on 9 June.

Louise came to Schonbrunn on 24 June, much distressed at reports of Franz's condition. Seeing him she burst into tears.

On 11 July 1832, Archduchess Sophie gave birth to a boy, Ferdinand Maximilian Joseph, who become the ill-fated Emperor Maximilian I of Mexico whom, before departing for Mexico[xxxvii], with the support of Napoleon III, declared himself the son of the Duke of Reichstadt. Prokesch recorded it was Sophie, among all of the Imperial Family, to whom Franz was closest in his last months.

That either would risk an affair was dubious. That Franz would have an affair with Melanie at the same time (also with Fanny Elssler) seems highly improbable.

On 21 July Malfatti advised the end was near. His mother and the Archduke Francis attended upon Franz's last rites. Franz passed away the following afternoon.

An autopsy conducted by Dr. Malfatti[xxxviii], Dr. Semlitsch, the Court Surgeon and Doctors Hieber and Rinna and Zungerl, house doctor to those at Schonbrunn

Palace, concluded that lung cancer was the cause of death.

It was reported his last words called for his mother. Baron Karl von Moll[xxxix], who was present, reported the event to Dietrichstein, away in Munich for the delivery of his daughter.

When rumours circulated in Vienna of the birth of a son fathered by the Duke of Reichstadt with a lady of the court, in July 1832 the only known child that fitted the description was the future Maximilian I.

Melanie's family could be relied upon to be discreet. Living in Vienna, their relatives and properties exposed to the wrath and power of the Habsburgs and the Romanovs, the child to be brought up in the hands of the Vatican[xl], themselves devout, they would not bring disaster on their heads or their dearest.[xli]

The death of the Duke of Reichstadt was covered by news sheets and gazettes everywhere, provoking an emotional outpouring. Louise was distraught.

On Franz's desk was a letter intercepted and delivered to Metternich: "If the presence of a nephew of your father, if the sins of a friend who bears the same name as you, could relieve your suffering a little, it would be the height of my wishes that I could be useful in something to one who is the object of all my affection." Its author was the future Napoleon III. If evidence were needed of the continuing devotion of his father's family, this was it.

Napoléon François Charles Joseph Bonaparte, variously Prince Imperial, King of Rome, Emperor of France, Duke of Reichstadt and heir to Napoleon I, was stifled in the manner of an exotic creature, forced by circumstances to live in a confined space, from whom all dreams, hope and opportunity were slowly plucked by those who found his very existence threatened their place in the world.

Just as he was smothered in life, so was his story controlled in death.

Emperor Francis (and his successors Ferdinand I and Franz Joseph I), Metternich, Dietrichstein and Prokesch, controlled the story with the power of the pen, publishing memoirs and reminiscences of the Duke.

No one who was not a member of the Habsburg family or one of its dependents was allowed sufficient access to the Duke in life nor to his writings in death to provide us with a picture that was not edited.[xlii]

In 1834, after successful performances in Berlin (where another old man, Friedrich Wilhelm III, King of Prussia, was said to have been smitten) and London, Fanny and Therese were invited to Paris by Dr Louis Veron, Director of the Paris Opera, who had travelled to London to judge them for himself. They agreed on a three-year contract. Back in Paris Veron set about organising advance publicity, stoking up interest in his new signings.

The owner of the daily theatrical newspaper 'Courrier des Theatres', Charles Maurice and he had often helped one another. The paper announced that "Something which has no bearing on the question, but will nevertheless do her much good, will add to the anticipated success of the Paris debut of one of the Mlles. Elssler. When this artist was appearing on the Vienna stage, people were curious to know whether she interested a prince who was very dear to the French nation and who died in the flower of youth to the sorrow of our age. Whether this rumour is well-founded or not, it is certainly one that will stimulate interest and curiosity in Mlle. Elssler. Whether it is seen only as an excuse for poignant memories, as a thought associated with so many cruelly disappointed hopes, or as an occasion...to express feelings which people who have not renounced their principles have for the illustrious dead, the opportunity will be seized to see and applaud her, and ponder."

Writers and critics picked up on the theme and the legend took hold. Fanny made no public comment, remaining firm in her private denials. Prokesch affirmed this, writing "what gave rise to these rumours was that the Duke's huntsman had sometimes been seen entering the house where Fanny Elssler was staying, but the huntsman was coming there because Herr Gentz and I had at that house a room which served us as a study or reading room, and this servant, certain of finding me there most often, brought me the short missives of the Duke, or came to request me to visit him".

It was a legend commercially astute and politically effective. It distracted from underlying realities, problematic ones. It was no accident that Fanny and Therese were invited to Berlin, to London and to Paris.

Fanny was sent away from Vienna and purposely exposed to the French public as the probable lover of the lost prince.

PART III - THE WARD

Melanie was spirited off to Rome, giving birth without fanfare. When the news of Franz's death came it must have been devastating. Whatever dreams they might have had were ended.

She would become a canoness, committed to a life of piety. So early in life her path was determined. She would live in the shadows, as would her child, a hostage.

We should not imagine that Melanie or her son (we will call him Alberto, though we are told he used the surname Kostrowicki)[xliii] were treated badly in terms of their daily needs. The Church has a long history of providing excellent tuition. We can expect that young Alberto Kostrowicki was given such an upbringing.

Alberto's 82-year-old grandmother, Letizia Bonaparte, Madame Mère, was resident in Rome, passing away four years later. Louise lived until 1847, when he was 16 years old.

With the Duke of Reichstadt gone, the rising hope of the Bonapartists became the able nephew of Napoleon I, now 24 years old, Charles-Louis Napoléon Bonaparte, son of Napoleon's younger brother Louis and of Hortense de

Beauharnais, the Emperor's stepdaughter, daughter of Josephine.

Elections held in December 1848 resulted in Louis-Napoleon Bonaparte, Franz's cousin, being voted in overwhelmingly as President (he secured more votes than all of the other candidates together).[xliv] Once again, a Bonaparte would lead France out of revolution, offering stability in uncertain times. Louis-Napoleon garnered support as the man who could stand above the political fray, under the mantle of the glory days when his uncle bestrode Europe.

He set about re-establishing order. The economy grew, witnessing significant development in industrialisation and development of railway communications. In December 1851, rather than face elections, Louis-Philippe lead a coup that saw him enthroned as Emperor Napoleon III.The Second Republic was at an end and the Bonapartes were restored.

In Russia, after the untimely death from typhus of Alexander I in 1825 (aged 47) he was succeeded by his brother Nicholas I, an autocrat and soldier, distrustful of the nobility (many of whom nursed grievances against Tsarist rule, impacting upon their privileges) and of political reform. It was a vast, mainly underdeveloped and backward country, with a middle class forming only slowly. In 1832 a secret police force was established (the 'Third Section'), overseeing a large network of spies and informers.[xlv]

Amidst the backdrop of these swirling events the career of Fanny Elssler continued to flourish. Fanny's appearances with the Ballet du Théâtre de l'Académie Royale de Musique (today the Paris Opera Ballet) were triumphant. She was an international star, much in demand. In 1840 Fanny and Therese sailed to New York, the first prima ballerina to visit the USA.

She was regularly seen dining in the company of John van Buren, the son of the President, returning with Therese to Europe in 1842, arriving in Liverpool on 28 July. She soon crossed paths again with Samuel Kostrowicki, Melanie's father.

Samuel had professed his love for Fanny in 1841. A limited edition of 100 copies were published in Brussels, under the title *Lettres à une artiste,* of extracts from correspondence in which the unnamed author disclosed he had met Fanny shortly after the death of Gentz.

Samuel would have considered himself in her debt. Fanny had sacrificed her reputation to protect his family. He asked her to retire from the ballet and to marry him.

In January 1843 Fanny made several diary entries revealing Samuel was pressing her for an answer and she was agonising over how to respond.

"6 January 1843 - (Proverb: When all else fails, faith, hope and love remain.) I slept peacefully, thanks to Thee, O Giver of all good things. I had a quiet day. I could experience so much if I complied with the wishes of one person. Is it my own will, or am I still blinded by the

glory of the world? I wish I could renounce this worldly glory. Yes, I believe I could, and am not afraid to admit it. In the evening I danced the *Cracovienne*; I was merry and so was the public. K. seemed calmer. At the end of this day I can truly say, "My God, I have faith, I love, and I have hope. Thanks be to Thee."

7 January 1843 - I have just received a letter from Reich. I expected more of him. Everyone seems to deceive me. Proven friends are the only ones one we should call friends, but it is difficult to find them. I have such a one at my feet. Why do I not accept him? Oh, Fanny, Fanny, take care, such things do not happen twice in a lifetime.

8 January 1843 - Today brought me only joy, no pain. After Church I met some friends. In the afternoon I saw K and talked about the future. How carefully he plans everything for me, like a father for his child. In the evening I was at Liszt's concert. I find him not natural, and much too calculating. This detracts greatly from his art. I did not enjoy it. I saw many people at the concert, and many people saw me. An empty evening.

12 January 1843 - I was uneasy the whole day. K wrote to me that I should not go to Strelitz. I replied that I must. Then I went to work, and saw K beside himself at my decision. In the evening I was alone with Minna and talked of all that had happened. She felt insulted that I had not confided in her. K had foreseen that it would turn out like this. I was wrong not to have spoken of it immediately. But who is right in this affair? I have proofs that K means well towards me. Can I doubt it? No. Then why this weakness, this doubt? Life no longer has any value for me. Everyone says he means well towards me, but nobody ever thinks of me, but only of him. Only God knows my heart, and only He can protect me. I trust in Him.

That day Fanny and her brother Johann learned the sad news of their father's death. They left Berlin to attend a requiem in Vienna, held in St Stephen's Cathedral. Fanny returned to Berlin for one more performance, before departing for London. Her father's death and the state of her relationship with Samuel were troubling her. Triumphant receptions of her performances at Her Majesty's Theatre and Covent Garden did much to relieve her.

In July 1843 we learn that Fanny, in Brussels for a five-week long tour, was invited to dinner by the Austrian Ambassador, Count Dietrichstein. Did he warn her off marriage with Samuel? Maybe, but it also seems likely that Fanny, long the object of attentions from powerful men wishing to possess her, enjoyed the self-determination and financial independence she had won and was not willing to subject herself to control by any man, however deep in her affections.

More years of performing in the capitals of Europe followed, until she decided to retire as she turned 41, performing 12 final appearances at the Kärntnertortheater in Vienna, the last on 21 June 1851. The whole of Viennese society wanted to see her, including Emperor Francis Joseph. Wealthy and independent, she settled in Hamburg.

While Alberto was growing up, Melanie lived in the shadows, dividing her time between Vienna and Rome, seeing her boy whenever she could. Samuel, provided, financed by his properties in Lithuania.[xlvi]

While her brother, Lucjan Kostrowicki[xlvii] was enrolled as a cadet at the French military academy at St. Cyr, Tsar Nicholas I visited. The Tsar's obsession with military matters and his love of parades was well known and the French arranged for him to inspect the Academy. The cadets were paraded before him and one of the Tsar's French hosts boasted that one of their best students was a Pole.

Fresh from crushing an uprising in Poland, Nicholas bristled. He considered himself the prime defender of ruling legitimism, proud of his nickname the "gendarme of Europe".

Nicholas saw France, and Paris in particular, as a hotbed of liberals and revolutionaries.[xlviii] After all, had not the contagion started here?

Now here at St. Cyr he faced a Polish nobleman from a family that had long taken part in fomenting resistance to his and his forebears' legitimate rule! On learning the identity of this student, Nicholas called for him to be presented, whereupon Lucjan found himself denounced as a traitor. Nicholas demanded he be released from the Academy and repatriated, with which the French authorities complied[xlix].

Once back at home at Papiernia, Lucjan was placed under house arrest, required to report to the police authorities regularly, forbidden to leave the country.

These disasters so upset their mother, Anna, that she left her daughters and husband in Vienna and returned to her family, the Zaleski's, in Volhynia.[l]

Fanny maintained her home in Hamburg, bringing up her daughter Therese until she was 21, in 1855, when she returned to live in Vienna, at an apartment at 14 Kärntner Straße, near to the Stephansplatz. Fanny's lively dinners and receptions were attended by a mix of old friends, of leading cultural lights and senior servants of the Empire. She was much loved by the city that had long since treated her as one of its own. Her beauty and style of dress barely adjusted over time. This quirk was part of her charm; others grew old, but not Fanny.

There she was in close proximity to Samuel Kostrowicki and his daughters. Fanny and Samuel remained close loving friends until his death in 1863, aged 75 (she only 53).[li]

Samuel purchased two neighbouring plots at the Hietzing Cemetery[lii]. One he kept for himself and his family, the other he offered to Fanny, so that they would be together eternally.

When in 1852 his uncle was crowned Napoleon III, Franz and Melanie's son, Alberto Kostrowicki became 21. We know as little of how he spent his days as we are meant to.[liii] By the time the Kingdom of Italy came into being he was 39 and Bonapartism was finished as a force in France. His mother, Melanie 58, Aunt Julia 59 and far away Uncle Lucjan 56. Fanny Elssler was a spritely 61 year-old.

Maurice Dietrichstein retired in 1845, living on to the age of 89, passing away in 1864[liv]. It was not until 1927 that Jean de Bourgoing would publish a collection of papers in book form entitled "Dietrichstein - Papiers Intimes et Journal du Duc de Reichstadt", comprised of letters, journal entries and other papers in the possession of the Dietrichstein family that belonged to or concerned the Duke. Dietrichstein had remained discreet to the end.

Clemens Metternich, whose long and distinguished career as Chancellor, in de facto control of the Austrian Empire, one of the key players in international events for more than three decades, was obliged to resign in 1848 over uprisings in Hungary and elsewhere in Habsburg domains. There was cheering in Vienna when his departure was announced – he had outstayed his welcome.

After years of exile, in Brighton, Metternich returned to Vienna in September 185 with the permission of Emperor Franz Jozef. Many senior figures who would play their parts in the years to come were interested to meet him. He passed away in Vienna in 1859, aged 86.

In 1872, when it was safe to assume the age of Bonapartism was well and truly over, Anton von Prokesch chose to publish, in Paris, his book entitled 'My relations with the Duke of Reichstadt' (*Mein Verhältniß zum Herzog von Reichstadt*). In 1871 Emperor Franz Jozef had appointed him Ambassador to The Sublime Porte[lv] and, in gratitude for 60 years of distinguished service, a hereditary count. He would live on until 1876.

PART IV - THE POET

Vienna, August 1880

A letter from Rome had been delivered, from her son. As she sat by the window in her outmoded salon gazing into the street, sipping at her morning cylinder of coffee, lost in reverie. Her surroundings reflected her life, vestiges of her Ruthenian roots and the style of a lost era, sparked by a Corsican who through genius and military prowess shook Europe over half a century earlier, but was not forgotten. Especially today.

Melanie's thoughts drifted across the years of careful silence. In this house she grew up. Happy, noisy, colourful days of discoveries and joy. Her dearest papa, Samuel and mama Anna, her sister Julia and brother Lucjan, of whom she had seen so little once he left for France, so many years ago, still a boy, and the impressive if austere elegance of the Imperial Court at the Hofburg and, in Summer, at magnificent Schonbrunn, in those days before everything changed. Louise and von Neippurg. The elegance of it all, the familiar formality, the wonderful lilting music, theatre, skating and later precious invitations to balls and soirees which began to

144

arrive after she was presented at Court by her proud parents to the Emperor and Empress. She was young, clever, well-educated and beautiful with life's promise before her, and so many dreams.

She had soon found to her heady delight she was attractive to men, but perhaps, as the daughter of an émigré, a political exile, a little too exotic and not what conservative aristocratic Austrian parents, concerned to advance their sons, would prefer. What young woman would not have been excited by those times? What old woman would not be warmed by occasional sweet memories? To have been beautiful and loved passionately and romantically, secretly, once in life is not offered to many women.

Most of all she thought about the glittering sensitive young man whom she had come to know, dared to love, won and so swiftly lost. Of what was and what might have been. Memories burnished over time, as she sat surrounded by mementos, his few possessions that had come to her.

A movement of flight caught her attention, broke the mood and brought her back. The years had made a realist of her very early. It was never possible, she understood as a mature woman, just as she had come to recognize this unbending reality most painfully many years ago.

The now tired elderly lady looked down at the letter in her hand and softly remarked "and so it begins again, poor boy". In this uncommon way did she greet the news that she had a grandson. Her own son was now nearly 50 years old and she had not entertained thoughts of his line continuing. A decade earlier, after Sedan, the chains had gradually slackened, but they were not free, they would never be free.

She was not the only reader of this letter or alone in knowledge of its delicate news. Letters between persons of interest that passed through the Imperial Postal Service were read, copied and re-sealed by the Secret Police, information reaching the authorities and even the Emperor, if need be, faster than the mail would reach her.

The anticipated birth of a child to Angelika de Kostrowitzky[lvi] (Olga) could not be ignored, due to the child's paternity.

The Imperial Chancellery informed the Emperor. This news was also relayed very discreetly through the most sensitive channels to the Heads of State and government of the major European Powers. All assured the matter was under control.

There was calm, the problem was now nearly fifty years old and had not come to light, the World had moved on, but not entirely.

In Vienna there was no doubt on the part of the Dyrektor of the Evidenzbureau[lvii] that the genie must remain firmly in the bottle. In his regular audience in the Emperor's study, where this hard-working man took a detailed and personal interest in the goings on across his vast empire and within his sometimes troublesome family, Emperor Franz Joseph had made it clear to him there must be no trouble. The Emperor had a long memory and an unforgiving nature. The Dyrektor knew his place, he was there to serve, effective and useful, not to fail.

Rome

They had met to discuss a dilemma. The now elderly, Antonio Saverio De Luca, Vice-Chancellor of The Holy Roman Church, Prefect of the Pontifical Congregation for Studies, Cardinal-Priest of San Lorenzo in Damaso and Cardinal-Bishop of Palestrina was tired. On days like this he regretted the complexity of his offices that usually and for many years had driven and sustained him, even though he was now well into his seventies. Before him sat a man, now of middle age, of still remarkable visage, a man whom he had known for decades, a man brought up in the shadows of the Vatican City and under the care of the Roman Church. Kindly affectionate care, but within limitations and supervision. That these factors had not prevented the events which brought them together again this morning had at first, months ago, come as a shock, now the challenges were tangible.

Thinking back to their first conversation on this matter, the Cardinal remembered that among the jumble of thoughts he first entertained was surprise that his visitor, now in his late forties, should after all of these years produce a child and, remarkably, that the mother, in her early twenties[lviii], many years his junior, should be his cousin (of sorts), albeit so distantly related as not to be more than curious (this was not unknown among noble, or for that matter even royal families)[lix]. And this was an extraordinary family, even its name meant "of the Cross", its ancestors "Lovers" and "Friends" of God.

It was the very fact that there had appeared to those monitoring Alberto to be nothing unusual in lengthy and regular visits to call upon his Kostrowicki cousins that had lulled them. They had not guessed at the relationship developing between this mature man and his much younger pretty cousin. Any other female interest would have been reported on, warned off. It had happened before. How could they have known?

His mind turned to the present. If this newly minted father were willing or even enthusiastic about denying paternity, and the mother not so stubborn, matters could be handled simply and traditionally. The child could be placed in an orphanage or found adoptive parents. That would be much the best outcome.

Strange, Antonio thought, that of all the pressing and complex matters of Church, State and Theology that sit upon my table, far away from my younger, simpler days in Sicily and as a priest in Monreale, I am drawn back into a matter of this kind, a pastoral, human, delicate and political matter. His visitor looked to him as his friend, in many respects his father, in place of the man he had never known, whose legacy, such as it was, had been denied.

His visitor coughed politely, and the Cardinal turned his gaze, for a few glazed moments trained out of the window of his large office in the Palazzo della Cancelleria and focused on him. "I suppose I must start by congratulating you. That would be usual. As you very well know, however, little that involves you is usual.

148

Certainly not this. As your friend I understand the loneliness that your restrictions have placed upon you. I am a priest and chose the life I have led. You had no such choices to make."

His anxious visitor replied "but surely we can lead together the quiet life here in Rome which I have always lived and complied with? Together we can bring up our son as I was brought up. Our secret remains safe, for the safety of my child even more than my own. You of all people should understand that. When he is an adult, he can live a normal life, without attention, nearly a century will have passed, and the World will have forgotten. I have asked for little, but this I ask for, I insist, I, I demand!", his emotion coming to the surface, pleading.

The Cardinal replied deliberately in his quiet measured tones that habitually never varied, "you are in no position to demand and I hope I need not remind you of the dangers for you and those close to you. Remember, I am your friend in this as in all things. Come again to see me in a few days. I will send for you. I must think and consult. Talk to no one; all depends on discretion. I will give you a final answer then."

Torn by his mixed emotions, love for Olga, for his new son Guillelmo and by his concerns and frail nascent hopes, Alberto returned slowly and thoughtfully to the apartment shared by Olga and her father, and now his new problematic grandchild.

Michael Apolinary Kostrowicki, Olga's father, a soldier by profession, was a Papal Chamberlain, receiving a small stipend[lx], and devoutly Catholic. Michael, his wife, Julia Floriani, and young Olga had emigrated to Rome in the 1860's, after the collapse of the 1863 Uprising, in which Michael Apolinary (then an officer in the Tsarist Army) and his brothers Jozef and Adam, with other relatives, had participated. Michael had escaped, but his brothers were marched to Siberia in chains. The family's property was confiscated.[lxi] They came via London, where her brothers Henri and Constantine remained.

In Rome they were grateful to find cousins. Alberto became a regular visitor to their home, where he could hear stories of his maternal Ruthenian roots. Several Kostrowickis had served in his grandfather's armies. The secret of his birth was known by some within the family. This household became a home, a place of refuge, for him and his mother, Melanie, during her visits to Rome. 'Family first'..

It was now a place of complex emotions. Very little heartfelt joy had greeted the new arrival, or earlier the revelation of this prospect. A pall hung over the place. These were damaged people living damaged lives. They were awaiting their sentencing. Powerless to intervene.

Not much distant, Colonel Karl Freiherr von Ripp paced uncomfortably and irritably before Antonio De Luca. Although he thought there were better uses for his time, he had come by train from Vienna to meet alone with the Cardinal. The Dyrektor of the Evidenzbureau had no illusions as to the security of the telegraph and postal communications systems between Rome and Vienna. His agency monitored them. They collected intelligence from various sources and put these into daily reports to the Chief of Staff and weekly reports to the Emperor. He knew interesting gossip fodder when he saw it.

In the preceding minutes the Cardinal had related the news, including the wishes of his ward.

"Your Eminence, this is a problem that we believed had been managed and, in a decade or two, perhaps sooner, would naturally and tidily end."

"Indeed Colonel, we are all responding to this unhappy change of circumstance. You have no doubt been apprised of the full situation by your predecessor, Colonel von Leddihn, including of the existence of certain longstanding sureties?"

Annoyed that the Prince of the Church seated in front of him should have casually questioned his access to sensitive matters touching on the Imperial Family, the Freiherr bristled. "What does the Church suggest, your Eminence?"

"The Church, indeed, the Holy See, has been a sanctuary, overseeing this situation these many years. The child became a man, and he caused no upset, no harm. Political foundations have not been challenged or shaken, despite the storms that blew abroad or even here in Rome. His mother and her family have sacrificed to support him. He has asked for little. Now he asks for his son. A son he did not expect but greets with understandable joy."

"Yes, yes, but come to the point please your Eminence",

the Colonel urged rudely. He wanted to get to his reserved cabin on the overnight train.

The Vice-Chancellor of The Holy Roman Church was not to be rushed, certainly not by a jumped up policeman. "Indeed, Colonel. Please do sit down," he urged. Colonel von Ripp looked closely into those orbs of dark Sicilian stone and sensed for the first time the inner strength of the man he was dealing with. Between the owner of those imperious eyes which bore into him weekly as he reported in a private study in the Hofburg or, more inconveniently, at Schonbrunn, and those of the Prince of the Church now contemplating him, the Colonel was coming to feel his options were limited, an uncomfortably deflating sensation for one usually handled with care, even fear, and not at all what he had expected as he travelled here and even when he arrived. Of course, he had not met Antonio De Luca before. De Luca's time as Apostolic Nuncio, or ambassador, to the Imperial Austrian Court had preceded his own elevation. von Ripp sat where indicated, looking at the Cardinal.

"Certainly, the initial news that there would be another generation was an unwelcome surprise. That was months ago, and we have had time to anticipate Signor Kostrowicki's state of mind and likely paternal affections and wishes. He is a lonely unfulfilled man of promise but with no outlet for its application. What else should we expect? He is not heartless, far from it, something of a romantic and probably why we are where we are and he is where he is, for that matter. It does appear that history is repeating itself, if you will pardon the use of the expression here [the Colonel's face sought to be disappointingly impervious]. He is also in love and with a lively young woman many years his junior. He imagines himself on the verge of a new life."

"Your Eminence, I really must insist...." He began, to be cut off. "Quite so, Colonel. You have to admit, however, that in all of this there is an extraordinary story fit for the theatre or even opera. Even Cardinals are allowed such occasional pleasures."

Having caused the Colonel's mind to heat, the Cardinal moved on. "So, let us be serious. Where we succeeded before we can succeed again", and with that the two eventually agreed upon a course that had worked before.

Before taking his leave the Dyrektor of the Evidenzbureau spoke. "Can you assure me that the Kostrowicki's will abide by this? It doesn't seem to me that Alberto is in a frame of mind to listen, as for the child's mother..."

De Luca replied "He will argue but he will come to agree. She will resist, with even greater passion at first, but she will agree more readily than him, because I can offer them something that they will truly prize" and, looking into the quizzical blue eyes of the Austrian policeman before him he added one word.

When later the evening train to Vienna pulled out of Rome, von Ripp sipped at a glass of chilled delicate Gavi di Gavi, sighed, examined the menu on the white and silver bedecked table before him and enjoyed the moving views of the City of Seven Hills, satisfied that his journey was worthwhile and that he could face the Emperor. He dined alone, secure in the knowledge that he had taken his own precautions. After all, from what he had learned through studying the chapters of this ongoing story, the women involved were not to be underestimated.

Vienna

At her bureau, by the window, in the mixed rays of the setting late Summer sunshine, warmed by the glow of gas lights only recently lit by her housekeeper, Melanie sat writing a short letter. It contained an invitation that would have unsettled von Ripp.

Over the course of the night before – she suffered from insomnia – and during the day she travelled back in her mind, running through broken images of events that shaped her life, that of her son and now would define her grandson.

She felt the unexpected beginnings of optimism. It brought the hint of a smile to the once beautiful face of this old lady who had had to be strong for so many years, for her son, for the father he had never known and with whom she had shared only a short, exciting, heady and frightening time, once she entered the 'gilded cage'.

Some are drawn to the flame where others draw back. It was in her blood and he recognized it, drew her in, willingly. Strength she only later learned she possessed. She loved from the first, a beautiful, clever, witty, talented caged bird. A young man who could shape events, crushed by the mantle of his inheritance. Tears fell.

Rome

Olga was angry and plain difficult and she was still feeling tired, sore and unwell, the cause of which was announcing himself with more noise, demands and regularity than she anticipated, despite voices of experience.

He had returned the day before in low spirits, hoping for understanding. She dis-abused him of the notion and he eventually spent a miserable night alone in his own rooms.

That Olga was fiery, intelligent and strong-minded was part of her appeal. He had watched her growing up. She was wonderful in a silken mood, could be gay and brilliant, but that was small comfort when the mercury dropped, clouds appeared and thunder and lightning followed, or worse, froideur, which she did very well.

Becoming a father had its exciting side, but it was dawning that the theory and practice were not aligned. His experience to date was the solitary life of a bachelor, but for the heady affair into which he found himself steadily, and then suddenly and deliciously drawn. He loved her of course and the boy, the wonderful boy, even more. He would have to fight - he had a cause! Something truly worthwhile. Thank God. It must be meant. Surely, they would agree.

Vienna

The following evening at precisely 9 pm the doorbell rang. Melanie open the heavy front door herself, her servants dismissed for the evening. Her maid, Agnieszka, had not thought to question the gift of a pair of tickets to the operetta. Her employer had long been kind; she was more of a companion, carer and even friend than a housekeeper. Another noble daughter of the East whose family had fallen on hard times, punished for standing up against the invader. Her loyalties firmly with Melanie.

There was only the low glow of an oil lamp in the hall, barely lighting the interior or the face of her visitor, unremarkably dressed in a well-cut black woollen overcoat and hat, having descended from the curtained black fiacre, typical of street cabbies (though closer examination by an expert in horseflesh of the dark potent animals that drew it would bely this picture), its stocky driver seated patiently. He knew what his master expected of him. Absolute discretion, unwavering vigilance, ready (and armed) when needed, anticipating danger, exciting no unwanted attention. An Empire might depend on it, an Emperor certainly did. He was proud of his job, as only a Guardsman can be. He loved his master, whom he had long watched over, as he was doing now, noticing everything.

With prying eyes shut out, Melanie curtseyed. Her Imperial caller removed his overcoat and hat, placed them on a hall chair with his cane and greeted her with the words: "I am here Madame." "Thank you for coming, Your Majesty. We are alone. Please come through." She indicated the door to her salon and without saying more they went into the heavily curtained room, to sit by the fire, facing one another. He did not accept the refreshment offered. He had no intention of staying.

The Emperor considered himself experienced at gauging those he met, a vital attribute. Briefed on events in Rome he believed he knew the subject matter to come. What else could have motivated her to write that she needed to speak to him in person on a matter touching on "L'Aiglon", a term he had not heard for many years, knowing he was not likely to refuse, much that he might prefer to. He sent back a brief handwritten note by the same messenger, also a Polish woman, who at his bidding was ushered to him and waited as he asked.

He now waited, regarded this elderly, still handsome woman, once beautiful to the point of turning the head of a king who never ruled. Franz Joseph (born not long before Alberto Kostrowicki) realized he was curious to meet her.

"Your Majesty I have disturbed you because I feel I must. I have news from my son. News that …" "you have a grandson, Madame", her guest completed the sentence. Melanie's eyes narrowed, "I have a grandson" she agreed. There was a pause, while Melanie took in the obvious conclusion that, as she anticipated, her mail was intercepted or, just as likely, the Emperor's information network still extended its interest to the affairs of her family, or perhaps both, he had chosen to remind her. They were in a web and its threads lead back to the autocrat in her salon.

"I have asked to see Your Majesty so that I may, for my son and my new grandson request, beg if that will help, as my son deeply desires, that they, with the child's mother, be allowed to live together in Rome as did I and my son those many years ago."

"Madame, you will have to pardon me for not greeting this newcomer with joy."

"Your Majesty know that if anything untoward happens to this baby boy his great-grandmother's instructions will be followed. His legacy and his loss will be made public in the broadest manner. He is to be protected as has my son been protected."

"You are very clear Madame. Impertinent, but very clear. We are in 1880, not 1820. Remember that."

"Memories are long. Your Majesty would not have come if my words have no meaning."

He made no promise, nor did he object. Melanie was wise not to press harder. She knew he would not be pushed by her to express a commitment, that like all men of great power and responsibilities, he could be dangerous and should not be provoked.

Without further meaningful communication he departed as he came.

Melanie returned to her salon and seated herself in her habitual chair. She was satisfied. He would not allow harm to come to her new grandson. Louise had seen to that long ago. She had not needed to remind him, she now knew. Warmed by this thought she mused and then slept until, an hour or so later, an excited Agnieszka returned with news of the evening's dramatic entertainment, oblivious of the visitor she had missed. Melanie told her to make hot chocolate for both of them and to sit down and tell her all about her evening.

Rome

Alberto was summoned to Cardinal De Luca. The judgment was what he had hoped for. They could be together, in Rome, only in Rome.[lxii]

Olga and the boy, Wilhelm, continued to live in Rome until 1887, when they moved to Monaco. We do not know for how much of this time Alberto was with them. Another son was born in 1882, named Alberto Zevini, father 'N.N.', not known and mother not named (hence 'Zevini', the name provided by the registrar, as was custom in such cases). In 1888 Olga 'recognised' Alberto, who was re-registered as Alberto de Kostrowitzky (later, in France, he dropped the 'o').

In South Africa, in 1879, a brave young man, a soldier brought up and educated in England died, his body pierced many times, by the hands of the Zulu enemies of Britain. Queen Victoria was deeply saddened, she had been very fond of Napoléon Eugène Louis Jean Joseph Bonaparte, Prince Imperial, the son and heir of Napoleon III, who moved to England with his family when his father was dethroned in 1870. When his father died in 1873 hopeful Bonapartists had declared him Napoleon IV, but of course this had not transpired. It was widely recognised as the end of any hope for the House of Bonaparte to rule in France again.[lxiii]

In Vienna, on 27 November 1884, Fanny Elssler, ailing in recent years, passed away, aged 74. Her body was interred at Hietzinger Friedhof Cemetery[lxiv], with a splendid gravestone, in that grave bought many years earlier by her late friend and would-be-husband, Graf Samuel Kostrowicki, Melanie's father. They would finally be side by side.

We do not know when Alberto Kostrowicki passed away. That Olga moved with her sons from Rome to Monaco in 1887 would be consistent with him being gone.

The Church had not forgotten them, nor various secular authorities, in Vienna and elsewhere. The Benedictine Order was close to the heart of the matter.

An old respected noble family, servants of the Vatican and of King Ferdinand II of the Two Sicilies, closely related and allied to the Habsburgs (his paternal grandmother was Maria Carolina of Austria, his second wife Maria Theresa of Austria) and therefore to Franz, supplied a cover story for Angelika and her sons as they moved to Monaco. It was a scandalous one - difficult for such a conservative family - but therefore all the more plausible. Francesco Costantino Camillo Flugi d'Aspermont[lxv] was already the black sheep of the family, a colourful adventurer. A little more colour would not make much difference, especially in a cause supported by his family, the Church and the authorities.

It was put about that Angelika had been Francesco's mistress and that, it could be inferred, her sons were by him - an aristocrat who lived for a time in Rome, with close links to the Church, whose brother, Dom Romarino Flugi (born Niccolo Flugi d'Aspermont), was General of the Benedictine Order. An order with strong affiliations with the Habsburgs and associated with the Bonapartes. From 1885 Francesco disappeared.

Angelika would, for a time, receive money from Dom Romarino[lxvi]. He arranged the education of Wilhelm and Albert by Marian Fathers in Monaco. Wilhelm excelled, remaining in Monaco until he moved to Nice early in 1897 to study for his baccalaureate. He lived in France for most of his life.

Angelika lived on, close to her sons. She would outlive Wilhelm (Apollinaire), but only just. Many colourful stories would be attributed to her.

AFTERWORD

Wilhelm Albert Włodzimierz (*Vwodzimierz*) Apolinary Kostrowicki revealed his identity. Wounded in 1916, he never fully recovered and passed away on 9 November 1918, a victim of the flu pandemic, aged only 38. He was interred in the Père Lachaise Cemetery, in Paris. He left his widow of one year, Jacqueline Kolb, but no children.

As Apollinaire died, so did empires - Austria, Germany, Russia, all swept away, their dynasties no longer relevant. We cannot know what more he might have felt free to reveal.

In 1916, contemplating his own mortality, Apollinaire, published *Le Poète assassiné* (The Murdered Poet), a collection of autobiographical poems, amongst which was *La Chasse à l'Aigle* (The Hunting of the Eagle)

'I had been in Vienna a week. It never stopped raining, but the weather was mild, midwinter though it was.

I made a special point of visiting Schonbrunn, and felt full of emotion as I walked in the dripping, melancholy park, once the haunt of the tragic King of Rome, fallen in rank, to be mere Duke of Reichstadt.

From the "Glorietta" - the name struck me as an ironic diminutive, one that must have made him dream of the glory of his father and of France - I stared a long time out over the capital of the Hapsburgs, and when night fell and all the lights came on I started to walk back towards my hotel in the centre of the city.

I lost my way in the outskirts, and after many false turnings I found myself in a deserted street that was wide and dimly lit. I caught sight of a shop, and dark though it was and seemingly abandoned, I was about to go in to ask my way, when my attention was attracted by another pedestrian, who brushed lightly against me as he passed. He was short, and a capelet of the kind worn by army officers floated from his shoulders. I quickened my steps and caught up with him. His profile was turned to me, and as soon as I glimpsed his features I gave a start. Instead of a human face the creature beside me had the beak of an eagle, curved, powerful, fierce, and infinitely majestic.

Concealing my agitation, I continued to walk ahead, staring attentively at this strange personage with the body of a human and the head of a bird of prey. He turned toward me, and as his eyes stared into mine a trembling, old man's voice said in German:

"Have no fear. I am not a bad man. I am an unfortunate."

Alas! I could make no answer, no sound came from my throat, it was so parched with anguish. The voice resumed, now imperious and with a hint of scorn:

"My mask frightens you. My real face would frighten you more. No Austrian could look at it without terror, because I know I look exactly like my grandfather..."

At that moment a crowd rushed into the street, pressing and shouting; other people came out of the shops, and heads peered from windows. I stopped and looked behind me. I saw that those who were coming were soldiers, officers dressed in white, lackeys in livery and a gigantic beadle who was brandishing a long staff with a silver knob. Some stable boys were running among them, bearing flaming torches. I was curious to know the object of their chase, and I looked in the direction they were headed. But all I could see before me was the fantastic silhouette of the man in the eagle mask, fleeing, his arms outstretched and his head turned as though to see what this danger was that was threatening him.

And at that instant I had a vision that was very precise and immensely moving.

The fugitive, seen thus from behind, his short cape spread wide over his arms, and his beak in profile above his right shoulder, was exactly the heraldic eagle in the armorial bearings of the French empire. That marvellous effect lasted barely a second, but I knew that I had not been alone or mistaken in what I had seen. The crowd pursuing the Eagle stopped, amazed by the sight, but their hesitation lasted no longer than the vision.

Then the poor human bird turned his beak away, and all we had ahead of us was a poor unfortunate, making a desperate effort to escape from implacable foes. They soon caught up with him. In the gleam of the torches I saw their sacrilegious hands catch hold of the cornered Eagle. He screamed some words that so filled me with panic and so paralysed me that I was incapable of even thinking of going to his help.

His last desperate cry was: "Help! I am the heir of the Bonapartes...."

But fists rained blows on his beak and on his head, and cut short his plea. He fell lifeless, and those who had just murdered him promptly raised him up and hurriedly bore him off. I tried to catch up with them, but in vain; and for a long time, at the corner of the street they had taken, I stood motionless, watching their flickering torches fade away in the distance....

A short time after that extraordinary encounter I attended an evening gathering at the home of a great Austrian nobleman whom I had known in Paris. There were marvellously beautiful women, many diplomats and officers. For a brief moment I found myself alone with my host, and he said:

"Everywhere you go in Vienna just now you hear the same strange story. The newspapers don't speak of it, because it is too obviously absurd to be believed by anyone with common sense. Still, it is something that cannot help interest a Frenchman, and that is why I want to tell you about it. People are saying that in a secret ceremony the Duke of Reichstadt married a daughter of one of our great families, and that a son born of this marriage was brought up unknown even to those in attendance at court. The rumour is that this very important person, the true heir of Napoleon Bonaparte, lived in concealment until an advanced age, and that he died barely two or three days ago in particularly tragic circumstances, though precisely how is not known."

I stood there silent, not knowing what to answer. And in the midst of the brilliant party I had a vision of the old Eagle who had spoken to me. Condemned to be masked for reasons of state, wearing the superb sign of an august race... Perhaps I had seen the son of the Eaglet."[lxvii]

In a letter dated 28 November 1958, Jan Kostrowicki, great nephew of Melanie (the grandson of her brother Lucjan (*Lutsian*)) wrote (in Polish)[lxviii]:

"It is understood that I fully comprehend the importance of explaining the lineage of Apollinaire - Kostrowicki and his relationship with the family and through him with Poland, however, what I can communicate to you will be only to report information that in 1903 or 1904 my father[lxix] told me when I was 15 and so it is very much what is still in my head. Nevertheless, I remember this story quite well, and I remember some fragments almost literally. I cannot, unfortunately, support my current statement with any material evidence, because all the family memorabilia in the form of documents, files, letters, memoirs, engravings, etc., was lost during the First World War; so my story will only allow speculation and supposition... and this will not constitute any historical value, unless you manage to obtain your direct or indirect evidence from the Austrian archives [and] access the material regarding the [Austrian] Court from the period covered by my story and an explanation of certain facts in the Vatican archives. Then it would be possible to see a lot of ambiguity about Apollinaire's pedigree.

Now to tell [about] my father and the events of the story [above]... A dozen or so years before the day when my father related this to me and my older brother, he visited his aunt..., Melanie Kostrowicka, already an old woman, living in Vienna in her own home on one of the main streets, the name of which I do not now remember. When my father inquired about this house, he was told that it was the palace of the Kostrowicki family, and that there lived not Frau Kostrowicka, but "die alte Grafin" (the high Countess). It surprised my father a little because he did not pretend to any title himself. However, my great aunt, Melanie, may have had grounds for using the title of countess, because soon after the death of my father, I received from my sister and my aunt a number of family documents, and among them the family tree. It was made on parchment a few hundred years earlier (the date that I saw on this document, today I do not remember) and it contained the signatures of Tsarina Catherine and Repnin[lxx], stating the family's right to the title of nobles and coat of arms (Bajbuza)(*Bybuza*). On this document there was an inscription declaring that "because the Kostrowickis were *comes* [lxxi] obviously, now they have the title of counts", then the date was visible (above the signature of Catherine) and the signature was illegible, though sweeping. This detail is given to you because it could have influenced the fact that my great aunt, Melanie, found herself at the Austrian court.

After this digression, I return to relating the story of my father's visit to his aunt in Vienna. His aunt received my father in a religious outfit, in a black habit with a large cross on her breast hung on a massive chain and with a red cap on her grey head. My father visited Aunt Melanie for a few days, they visited the cemetery [at Hietzing], where the Kostrowicki family grave was located. Melanie's parents and her sister were buried there. Also buried there was Fanny Elssler, a famous Viennese ballet dancer, but about her later.

The house - the palace where my father's aunt lived, was richly furnished, my aunt Melanie had numerous servants, such as a porter, a butler, several ladies' maids, she had to be wealthy. One can guess that the visit of my father was aimed not only at family responsibilities, but also at hopes of inheritance.

Aunt Melanie bestowed upon…my father several portraits of her, her father and sister and her grandfather and some of ancestors in armour with shaved heads[lxxii]. The portraits were well brushed, I can confirm this, because I studied painting for several years. There was also a well done painting of St. Francis, the face of this saint gave an impression that was similar to the likeness of Fanny Elssler, with the expression of the eyes and lips clearly betraying an irreligious smile. My father's portraits were placed in a few old-fashioned trunks, oddly shaped, covered in leather and intricate ironwork and copper. The trunks contained a mass of correspondence, documents, several items with engravings, drawings, watercolours, and quite a lot of oil paintings not bound, but rolled on wooden batons; on many of them on the reverse side were the inscriptions "King of Rome" or "Duke of Reichstadt", there were also copies of paintings from The Sistine Chapel, especially the head of St. Peter, which was probably the best copy of the original. There was some lace in the trunks, pretty shawls, and even shoes similar to those worn by dancers today. By donating these things, Great Aunt Melanie expressed her desire to remove from her eyes what she associated with the world that reminded her not only of the joyful past, but also of ill-fated experience. Beside this, my father's Aunt Melanie blessed him with the words: "God bless you, my angel," but she did not make any more concrete wishes. After her death, it turned out that both her capital and the palace were designated for St Peter's [Rome].

Father brought home the gifts he had received. The portraits were hung in the rooms of the house in the Koscieniew[lxxiii] property (*Koshcheniev*) in Wilenszczyzna (*Vilenshchina*), and the trunks with their contents were stored in a special locked space in the attic of the house.

Koscieniew was the property of my Uncle Samuel, father's brother, who lived in Riga permanently (he was the chief architect there), and my parents (my sister and brother) spent our holidays there[lxxiv].

When I and my brother asked my father about the lives of our great aunts Melania and Julia and our grandfather (and their brother) Lucjan and their parents, my father told us the following stories. Our great-grandfather Samuel, the father of the above-mentioned Melanie, Julia and Lucjan, was the son of Ignacy Kostrowicki (*Ignatsy Kostrovitski),* General of Artillery in the Polish Army, participant in Napoleon's Moscow campaign.[lxxv] He had the following properties in the Vilnius region: Kowale, Papiernia and Koscieniew (*Kovale*), as well as some properties in Polesie, but I do not remember their names. He married a lady from the Volynskaya region[lxxvi], Miss Zaleska, a wealthy and intelligent person.

Political accidents that occurred in Poland at that time probably caused my great-grandparents to travel to Vienna, where they acquired the house where my father visited my great aunt.

My great-grandparents had three children - two daughters, Melanie and Julie, and a son Lucjan, my grandfather. They gave all of their children a careful and comprehensive education, and therefore knowledge of foreign languages, literature, music, painting, and my great aunt [Melanie] demonstrated many talents. When my great-grandfather's children reached the appropriate age, my great-grandfather sent my grandfather to France, to the Higher Military School[lxxvii], and his daughters were accepted at the Austrian Court, where they entered the circle of Marie Louise, wife of Napoleon I, who after the French Empire fell had returned with her son, the Duke of Reichstadt, to her parents...

My great aunts, besides being well mannered, were, based on their portraits, very beautiful and handsome, especially Melanie. Here the secret of her life and fate begins. According to my father's words, my great aunt at the age of 18 became pregnant[lxxviii]. This accident befell not only her parents but also the court of Vienna; however, the affair was not exposed, and Melanie was secretly sent to Italy, where the birth took place. She gave birth to a son who wore her name, and his given name my father did not want to disclose, nor did he want to reveal the supposed father of that child. When we asked him about this, my father answered that we were too young to understand the situation properly; he hinted that it was a high-ranking person associated with the throne of France.[lxxixlxxx]

That he was not a regular mortal, can be inferred [from the fact that] my great aunt's son grew up in the care of the Vatican, and the mother of the child often stayed in Italy. It is from that time that her paintings come, copies of paintings to be found in St. Peter's Basilica in Rome."

Jan Kostrowicki first learned of this story from his father in 1903 or 1904, living in what was then a dominion of Tsarist Russia.

Melanie, born in 1813, passed away in 1889 (the year in which Jan Kostrowicki was born). She was buried at Hietzing in the same plot as Fanny Elssler, next to that of her family . Marcin Kostrowicki, Jan's father, son of Melanie's brother Lucjan (who had died in 1867), living at Koscieniew, learned that he would not receive the 'Kostrowicki Palace' in Vienna, visited by him, nor indeed its contents or any other property from his Viennese relatives, save for those curiosities, boxes, papers, portraits, paintings, maps and other items, some bearing references to the erstwhile King of Rome or Duke of Reichstadt, that his Aunt Melanie had sent back home with him, now kept at Koscieniew.

In his letter of 28 November 1958[lxxxi] to Anatol Stern, Jan Kostrowicki explained that, his father having died in 1905, he and his brother Stanisław learned no more from him. The boys were sent away to school. Jan wrote that there were numerous documents, including letters in trunks that his father had brought back from Vienna to Koscieniew. Access to them was difficult, because only a few years after their father's death, he and his brother were sent off to school, and their stepmother and her relations remained at Koscieniew.

It was not until 1914, when the German army occupied Poland, and their stepmother had left for the Lublin region to go to her parents, that he and his brother remained and, even though they now had access to Great

Aunt Melanie's memorabilia, there was no time to read the documents and letters. Instead, the brothers packed these mementos, including all of the portraits, pictures, prints, engravings and drawings, into strong sealed chests so that at any time they would be easier to hide or move.

In 1914, the Tsarist Russian Army chose Koscieniew as their staff headquarters. Jan and his wife were allowed to stay in the manor house, living in one room. His brother Stanisław was managing the estate (of approximately 1,000 ha.) of their uncle, Wincenty Sieklucki, at Strzelica[lxxxii] Uncle had left the house and gone to join their stepmother (he was married to her sister, Felicja Nowakowska).

The Russians told him to remove anything of value. All valuables, carefully and securely packaged, were moved to Strzelica, which lay on the side-lines of communication roads, among swampy lakes and forests. They hoped their possessions would be safe there. News from the front and from areas under German occupation soon had them worrying. The retreating Russians were destroying everything, leaving nothing behind them. The Germans were plundering anything of value and repatriating what they took to Germany.

The Russian forces were falling back to the River Niemen, where they intended to hold a new line and halt the German advance - Strzelica would be overrun. Responding to these rumours, Stanisław decided to take all of the portraits to Sieniezyce[lxxxiii], a property belonging to another of their relatives (Stanisław Jundziłł[lxxxiv]) , behind the intended Russian lines. He also, alone, took all of the remaining chests of items and buried them in the Strzelin forest.

Jan found that although he had fulfilled his military service obligation and should not have been required to do so he was ordered by the Chief of Staff of the Russian Army Corps operating there to prepare to leave with the staff. Despite protests and holding the relevant discharge papers he had to comply.

The result was that at the end of the Summer of 1915 Jan and his wife, each driving a cart, were obliged to leave Koscieniew in the middle of night, taking only some personal items and food. They were not trusted by the Russians and their carts were parked later in the midst of a large staff camp. It was not until the staff departed for Minsk that they were able to leave.

Stanisław Kostrowicki had remained at Strzelica. He suffered under the German occupation and died in 1918. The German forces were not held at the Niemen and soon seized Sieniezyce, from where they stripped everything of value, including the portraits brought from Koscieniew for safety, sending these back to Germany to an unknown destination.

Jan wrote to Stern that "when, after the end of the war, I returned to Koscieniew, I did not find my brother of course, and the people in Strzelica[lxxxv], although they knew about my brother's removal of the chest (with files and other things), they could not point out where all of this was hidden. So all traces that can cast light on Apollinaire's interest [for us] have disappeared for now."

It is possible that, whether through investigative research or quirks of fate, some of the missing items, including those that were once the precious mementos of Melanie Kostrowicka and Franz, Duke of Reichstadt, may in time be found in Germany, in Belarus or elsewhere.

---

[i] Alexandre Florian Joseph, Count Colonna-Walewski (born 4 May 1810; died 27 September 1868).

[ii] Lucien Bonaparte, fell out with Napoleon, tried to escape to America, was captured by the British and well treated in Britain, where he was seen as anti-Napoleon, being allowed to live comfortably with his family at Ludlow and later in Worcestershire, until he returned to France in 1814.

[iii] He wrote in French (the diplomatic language of the age) *"Altesse royale, en butte aux factions qui divisent mon pays et à l'inimitié des plus grandes puissances de l'Europe, j'ai consommé une carrière politique, et je viens, comme Thémistocle, m'asseoir au foyer du peuple Britannique. Je me mets sous la protection de ses lois que je réclame de votre altesse royale comme du plus puissant, du plus constant et du plus généreux de mes ennemis. Ile d'Aix, 13 juillet 1815. Napoléon".*

[iv] Savary, one of the last to leave the Emperor on his abdication in April 1814, was among the first to welcome his return from Elba. From Plymouth he and Lallemand were taken to Malta and imprisoned ("interned"). They escaped after two months. Savary made his way to Smyrna. In financial difficulties, he travelled. He was permitted to return to France, settling later in Rome. After the July Revolution (1830) he was

rehabilitated and commanded a French army in Algeria.

Lallemand made his way back to England. In Liverpool, together with another French officer, he was smuggled on board an American merchant vessel, the Triton. They were then moved by small boat from ship to ship to avoid the British authorities, boarding and inspecting vessels and their rolls. They arrived in Boston in April 1817. Lallemand became president of the French Emigrant Association, which obtained a grant of four townships in Alabama for a vine and olive company. Rumours circulated that Lallemand would attempt to rescue Napoleon and put Joseph on a throne in South America. He returned to France after the July Revolution of 1830, serving as military governor of Corsica (1837-1838).

[v] Aside from two wives, more than 20 mistresses have been recorded; he was often financially generous toward them.

[vi] A French officer who had met Schulmeister wrote: "I was curious to see this man, of whom I had heard a thousand marvellous tales. He inspired the Viennese with as much terror as an army corps. His physique is in keeping with his reputation. He has a bright eye, a piercing glance, his countenance is stern and resolute, his gestures are abrupt, and his voice is sonorous and strong. He is of middle height but very sturdy…of a full-blooded temperament. He has a perfect knowledge of Austrian affairs and his portraits of its leading personalities are masterly. On his brow there are deep scars, which prove that he has not run away from dangerous situations. He is generous too: he is bringing up two orphans whom he has adopted."

[vii] Schulmeister made various attempts at new business ventures, each of which failed. He eventually acquired a

tobacco shop in Strasbourg, through a friend, where he lived out a quiet life, in full view of the watchful authorities. He died in 1853.

viii Joseph Bonaparte, Napoleon's elder brother, formerly King of Naples and Sicily (1806 – 1808) and King of Spain (1808 – 1813).

ix Gourgaud remained an ardent and loyal supporter of his patron. He became an active member of the Bonapartist Party until 1830. Rehabilitated (Commander of the Artillery in Paris (1830), appointed Lieutenant General (1835), made a Peer of France (1841), he was among those who returned to St Helena in 1840 to accompany Napoleon's body on its return to France. He then sought to include de Montholon in this mission, but unsuccessfully – de Montholon was imprisoned at the time. With Louis Napoleon (later Napoleon III)), Gourgaud attended the interment of Napoleon at Les Invalides (along with an estimated one million others who turned out on the streets of Paris for this momentous spectacle).

x Marchand kept a meticulous written record in the form of a diary. This was published for the first time in 1955. He also kept hairs from the head of the dead Emperor, shaved off his corpse a day after his death on St Helena. Scientific analysis indicated substantial doses of arsenic over a long and intermittent period. This has been disputed.

xi Louis-Joseph Marchand subsequently married Mathilde Brayer, daughter of Napoleonic General Michel Silvestre Brayer. He was confirmed as a count by Napoleon III in 1869 and admitted to the Order of the Legion d'Honneur.

xii The French writer and poet Auguste Barthelemy sought to

meet the Duke to present his own latest work. Count Maurice Dietrichstein was charged by the Duke's Grandfather, Emperor Francis, and by Metternich with overseeing the upbringing, security and affairs of the Duke; in effect he was his gaoler and keeper, responsible to the Emperor and his chief counsellor. Dietrichstein refused permission for Barthelemy to meet the Duke. This prompted Barthelemy to compose the poem 'Le Fils de l'homme" and to coin the the concept of an Eaglet in the Golden Cage of Schonbrunn Palace.

[xiii] The Dietrichstein Family owes its wealth and position to its long service and devotion to the Habsburgs, to whom they are related. Siegmund von Dietrichstein (1484 – 1533) was elevated to the noble rank of Freiherr by Emperor Maximilian I and purchased Hollenburg Castle in 1514. Siegmund married the Emperor's illegitimate daughter Barbara von Rottal (1500 – 1550), and he was said to have been favoured by the Emperor as a son. Siegmund and Barbara's great-granddaughter, Regina von Dietrichstein (d.1630) was married (2nd voto) to Kryštof Adam Vencelík z Vrchovišt a na Třešťi (d.1626). Maria Waleria Wentzl (1854 – 1937), wife of Ludwik Antoni Moczarski vel Mocarski, was from the well-known Polish Wentzl Family, patrician Krakow merchants and bankers, descended from the Vencelík z Vrchovišt a na Třešťi Family, from Bohemia.

[xiv] Born in Hungary to a family of Saxon aristocratic origins, he was a Dominican friar and military chaplain. In 1817 he became the confessor of Marie Louise and worked to regularise the cohabitation between her and von Neipperg. He received various honours and became Bishop of Parma in 1843 but was unpopular with both the local clergy (he was intransigent) and the local population (he was seen as an

Austrian stooge).

^{xv} Worth vastly more today.

^{xvi} In 1854 an additional $8 million was allocated to fulfilling the testamentary dispositions of Napoleon.

^{xvii} Barings had had a longstanding acquaintance with Napoleon. In 1802, Barings and Hope & Co. (as it then was) facilitated the Louisiana Purchase (the largest land purchase in history). This was done (with political support in London) even though Britain was at war with France, and the sale helped to finance the French war effort. After a $3 million down payment in gold, the remainder of the purchase was made in United States bonds, which Napoleon sold to Barings through its partner Hope & Co. of Amsterdam. Alexander Baring, working for Hope & Co., first made the arrangements in Paris and then sailed to the United States to collect the bonds and then back to deliver them to the French Treasury.

^{xviii} In the years after Waterloo and the restoration of the Bourbons and many returning ancien regime aristocrats, reclaiming lands and privileges, settling scores nurtured in exile, memories of the Revolution still recent, France experienced exhaustion from war, foreign occupying armies on its soil, unemployment, mechanisation (with consequent effects on the countryside, workers and their families paid meagrely and living in poor declining conditions), a bourgeoisie enjoying the products of industrialisation, but fearful of radicalism and social discontent. The Army felt disenfranchised, officers unhappy in peacetime, their own finances dwindling. These were circumstances ripe with discontent; that caused many to look back favourably upon the days of Empire and the regime of Bonaparte - a new cult of

Bonapartism developed. Images of the Emperor and of the Eaglet began to appear, sometimes disguised craftily, on canes, inside snuff boxes and elsewhere.

Art, music and literature picked up on the Bonapartist theme, a romantic, seductive theme, offering a better world to the oppressed and disappointed, the downtrodden and, elsewhere in Europe, those feeling the weight of the yoke of power, conquest and subjugation.

The news of Napoleon's death on St Helena in 1821 produced a massive literary and artistic reaction, with huge public appetite in France and elsewhere for the Napoleonic genre. This was the death of the modern Alexander, Julius Caesar, or Hannibal - the great commander and conqueror of modern times. A man who's most enduring legacy, transcending his many and great victories and devastating defeats, was the product of his visionary, ambitious, energetic breadth of concentration and innovation on more peaceful matters - on the legal system (the Napoleonic Code), governance, education, commerce, science and culture. A legacy that lives on. He changed our world, irrevocably and in many respects, for the better.

[xix] In 1853 Petrucci revealed this secret and testified that Revard was Napoleon I. It was safe to do so - in 1852 Napoleon's nephew, Louis-Napoleon, had ascended to the French throne as Napoleon III.

[xx] In 1872, there were published in Paris Anton von Prokesch-Osten's memoirs of his time with the Prince, entitled 'My relations with the Duke of Reichstadt' (translated from the original german into french as 'Mes Relations avec le duc de Reichstadt', edited and re-published by Jean de Bourgoing in

1925). This was two years after the decisive German victory at The Battle of Sedan, that resulted in the fall of the Second French Empire, the surrender, capture, and abdication of Napoleon III and the end of Bonapartism. It was published with official sanction, by the then elderly career diplomat, soldier and author, heavily rewarded by the Austro-Hungarian Crown, to which he had remained a grateful and loyal servant throughout.

It painted a kind but insipid picture of the prince, loved by his Austrian family and loving of his grandfather, Francis, willing to be a king, but only if the pathway were clear, with popular and official support and with the approval of his grandfather. A picture calculated to deflate any remaining Bonapartist talismanic reverence for this previously romantic figure. It largely succeeded.

These impressions were reinforced by the publication of the "Intimate Papers and Journal of the Duke of Reichstadt" kept by Count Dietrichstein - itself translated into french, then edited and published by J. de Bourgoing in 1927. Censorship is an old concept. In the words of Dietrichstein, Prokesch was an "assiduous [agent] of Metternich and Gentz" who supported his advancement. Gentz wrote "what Prokesch got on ten different occasions is fabulous".

xxi Prince Eugene of Savoy (1663 – 1736) a general and statesman of the Holy Roman Empire and the Archduchy of Austria and one of the most successful military commanders in modern European history.

xxii The Polish–Russian War / November Uprising (1830–31), was an armed uprising in the centre of partitioned Poland, the heart of Europe, against the Russian Empire. It was started in

Warsaw on 29 November 1830, when the young cadet officers attending the military academy of the Army of Congress (the proud rump of that army that once fought for Napoleon) rose in revolt. They were soon joined by large segments of Lithuania, Belarus and western parts of the Ukraine, all parts of the former Polish-Lithuanian Commonwealth (Rzeczpospolita). Despite some smaller successes, the uprising was eventually crushed by the much larger, better equipped and organised Russian Army of Tsar Nicholas I, who decreed that henceforth Poland was an integral part of Russia. Further repression followed.

[xxiii] The Rzeczpospolita was the Crown of the Kingdom of Poland and the Grand Duchy of Lithuania, after 1791 the Commonwealth of Poland, the confederation of Poland and Lithuania, ruled by a common monarch, who was both the King of Poland and the Grand Duke of Lithuania. It was among the largest and most populous countries of 16th Century and 17th Century Europe.

[xxiv] The upheaval in France that saw the overthrow of Charles X and the opportunity seized by Louis-Philippe to seize the throne was, perhaps, a missed opportunity for Franz to return as Napoleon II. As his father foresaw, his absence and captivity in the hands of Metternich were near insurmountable handicaps. The French people (and other nations) did not want war, as memories were still raw, even though many felt keenly the disaster of 1815. The inability of Bonapartists to communicate directly and effectively with Franz negated his opportunity. Metternich concluded that even placing a pro-Austrian Napoleon II on the French throne would upset the recently established balance of power in Europe.

[xxv] At the invitation of Emperor Francis, the Bourbons moved

to Prague in late 1832/33. After Francis died in March 1835, the Bourbons left Prague Castle, moving initially to Teplitz. Kirchberg Castle was eventually purchased for them.

xxvi It was a hopeless and tragic affair. Tsar Nicholas' uncle, the Grand Duke Constantine, Governor of Poland, demonstrated his disregard for the Polish Constitution, upsetting many Poles, including large segments of the Army's officer corps. It was the discovery of a Russian plan to employ Polish troops, in clear violation of the Polish Constitution, to put down the July Revolution in France and the revolution in Belgium that triggered revolt. Napoleon had offered a pathway to freedom and the restoration of an independent Polish Kingdom - many Poles and Lithuanians served and fought valiantly, died in his ranks to further this cause - and once again there were cries for a Napoleon in Warsaw - "Long live Napoleon II, King of Poland".

xxvii The Mayerling Affair (involving the mysterious death of Crown Prince Rudolf and his young lover Baroness Marie Vetsera in 1889), would in time shed light on what steps touching on the House of Habsburg were on occasion deemed necessary.

xxviii By Count Anton von Prokesch-Osten.

xxix To Rahel von Varnhagen, a friend.

xxx After Gentz's death Fanny was soon consoled in the arms of Anton Stuhlmuller, dancing by her side in Vienna and then Berlin, where Fanny, Therese and Anton went to appear in the Autumn. In Berlin they had a brief passionate affair, resulting in a daughter born in Edinburgh on 26 October and cared for, for a time by Mrs Grote, with whom she stayed when the sisters visited London to perform, arriving in April 1833. In London Fanny was introduced to Count Alfred d'Orsay, and soon there were rumours of another affair. Fanny attracted rumours.

xxxi Dubrovnik, Croatia.

xxxii From medieval times communities of secular canonesses were formed in which unmarried daughters and widows of the nobility could lead pious lives of devotion in relative comfort, with servants available, remaining free to marry, as some did. Some remained in their own homes. It was a form of retreat, without taking irrevocable vows. Such communities continue today.

xxxiii see p. 166, "Napoleon II" by Jean Tulard (pubd. by Fayard, 1992 ISBN 978-2-213-02966-5).

xxxiv We may speculate as to why Dietrichstein would leave us this confirmation, when so much else was done to cover over or divert from what occurred.

xxxv During the Congress of Vienna he enjoyed an excellent reputation and became the personal physician of Archduke Karl and Archduchess Maria Beatrice d'Este of Modena. On 31 December 1821 he married Polish countess Helena Ostrowska (1794–1826). The mother-in-law of Dr. Ambrozy Samuel Kostrowicki was Aleksandra Ostrowska (d.1919), wife of Albert Wojciech Boguszewski.

xxxvi In 1850 Frederic Chopin published love letters, 'from the Duke of Reichstadt to his cousin'.

xxxvii The Mexico adventure did not go well for him, he was later deposed and executed by firing squad.

[xxxviii] On 10 April 1837 Malfatti was awarded the title of Count of Monteregio for his contributions to medical science. Malfatti founded the society of general practitioners in Vienna in 1802. He was buried in the Heitzinger cemetery. The *Malfattisteig* in Hietzing is named for him.

[xxxix] A statesman and naturalist.

[xl] That the Vatican would assist in this matter touching so delicately on the Emperor's family was obvious. Francis had, until 1806, been the last Holy Roman Emperor, promoter and defender of Christianity, and the Roman Church. He and his relatives ruled over much of Italy and the Papal States were his neighbours. Louise's mother was the late Maria Theresa of Naples and Sicily (an Italian Bourbon). Church and State had long worked closely together, including in such sensitive matters; indeed, there had been speculation that Franz would, as a small boy, be handed over the Church for his upbringing, care and protection, but Francis had chosen to keep him in sight, at court. To have done otherwise would have antagonised the Bonapartists and potentially and unacceptably exposed the boy to kidnap or rescue, depending upon perspective. Louise probably interceded on her son's behalf.

Franz's own son was now destined for the alternative upbringing to which he himself might have been exposed, but in his son's case, in secrecy, his identity masked. The Vatican was expert in maintaining secrets - and it had no interest in a revival of the Bonapartes, especially fomenting unrest in Italy, where its temporal control in the Papal States was challenged.

[xli] Melanie's parents and sister lived out much of their lives in Vienna, close to the court. Graf Samuel Kostrowicki, the father, was involved in Polish cultural matters, becoming

President of the Polish PEN Club[xli]. He (in 1863) and later Julia and Anna Kostrowicka were ultimately buried in a Kostrowicki family plot in Hietzing Cemetery[xli] (purchased by Samuel), close to Schonbrunn Palace, maintained to this day by public funds.

[xlii] The Emperor and Metternich had possession of the Duke's papers and personal effects. Jan Kostrowicki recorded for us, as related to him by his father, her nephew Marcin Kostrowicki, that (in the late 1880's) Melanie was in possession of items of the Duke of Reichstadt's property, papers and effects that she gave to him to take back to the Kostrowicki family home at Koscieniew. Surely, these items could not have reached Melanie or been held by her without the knowledge and sanction of the Imperial Court, reflecting and respecting the wishes of the Duke and trusting that she and her family would abide by the accommodation that had been made, an arrangement that appears to have held until 1916.

[xliii] Marcin Kostrowicki passed away in 1905 without disclosing the boy's given name to his young sons.

[xliv] In Britain, France and Russia, the next two decades would witness simmering social tensions and change. The 1832 Reform Act saw enfranchisement extended beyond landowners to include any man paying taxes of £10 or more each year (over £1,000 today). The British model, and that of the USA, were watched closely in Continental Europe, with fear and suspicion by the autocrats and with some envy by the liberals. In 1830 Charles X issued the Four Ordinances of St Cloud, abolishing freedom of the press, reducing the electorate by three quarters and dissolving the lower house of the French Parliament. The resulting uproar, the Three Glorious Days of 26 - 29 July 1830, brought about Charles' abdication and the

installation of another Bourbon, from the Orleans branch, Louis Philippe, giving rise to the so-called July Monarchy.

Louis Philippe was a very wealthy and successful businessman, among the richest men in France. His policies were more liberal and supported by the petite bourgeoisie and bankers, railroad developers, owners of coal and iron ore mines, forests and landowners. Opposition to his regime came mainly from the ultra-royalists (who regarded him haughtily as an upstart) and from industrialists and working classes, unlikely bedfellows all. Enfranchisement favoured the landed classes, to such an extent that by 1848 only approximately one per cent. of the population could vote, alienating many people who were not necessarily natural allies.

The King became viewed increasingly as detached from the concerns of broad sections of the people. Pointing to the British model, encouraged by the free press, a mood of republicanism took root. A financial crisis (in 1846), failed harvests and rising unemployment, inflation impacted bread prices and, together with corrupt government practices, became the fuel of revolution. Fundraising banquets replaced illegal political gatherings until even these were outlawed.

On 22 February 1848 the citizens of Paris rose, flooded the city's streets and demanded reform and the removal of Louis Philippe's chief minister, Francois Guizot. The citizenry erected barricades and fought with the municipal guards. Guizot resigned the following day, but the angry crowds were unappeased. In a melee before the Ministry of Foreign Affairs soldiers fired on the pressing crowd, resulting in 52 deaths. The consequential anger turned on the King. With the crowds descending on his palace Louis-Philippe abdicated in favour of a small boy, his nine year-old grandson and, disguised, fled to

England.

A Second Republic was declared, but that year would continue to witness upheaval and frenetic political debate and activity, workers riots, xenophobia, elections, radical calls for an international crusade for democracy, even calling for the restitution of an independent reunited Poland (where an uprising had started on 20 March - the Wielkopolska Uprising). The middle classes, fearful of a workers' revolt and all that could follow, pressed successfully for the Army to restore order, ultimately achieved by some 120,000 troops overcoming the barricades that had blockaded Paris. It was a victory, but it had driven a lasting wedge between the working classes and the bourgeoisie.

[xlv] Having had experience of crushing and subjugating the Poles in 1830, Nicholas I responded resolutely to the call for aid that came from Franz Joseph I of Austria in 1849. An uprising in Hungary, determined to throw off the Austrian and Habsburg yoke, was winning ground, measured in victories over Franz Joseph's forces.

Nicholas sent a powerful force of 280,000 men (200,000 regulars and 80,000 auxiliaries), that, together with Austrian forces, crushed the hopes of the Hungarians (and of many others contemplating action). Hungary would remain, resentfully, under Habsburg rule until the aftermath of WWI.

The succession of the more liberal minded Alexander II in 1855 brought with it some reforms (in government, the military, in education and in the legal system and notably the emancipation of serfs in 1894). His assassination in 1881 - a bomb thrown under his carriage having caused extensive and horrible injuries, he bled to death, witnessed by members of his family - brought swift reaction. Alexander III, his son, cracked down on dissidents, strengthened the security police and addressed the situation of the peasants and workers, extending land ownership rights and worker protections (limitation of working hours, proscribing child labour, etc.), and encouraged industrialisation.

[xlvi] His landholdings included some 17,000 hectares.

[xlvii] Letter to Anatol Stern from Jan Kostrowicki dated 28 November 1958 - see pp. 218 - 229, "Dom Apollinaire'a", by Anatol Stern.

[xlviii] After the collapse of the November 1831 Uprising some 5,000 Poles fled to France, mainly Paris. Among these were not only displaced aristocrats and political leaders, but intellectuals and important cultural figures such as Mickiewicz and Chopin. Poles considered France was morally in their debt, due to their support for Napoleon and their recent resistance to autocratic rule - to Nicholas.

[xlix] It would be reasonable to assume that the French intelligence service knew of Lucjan's Viennese family connections; perhaps also that he was the uncle of a well-connected child in Rome; related to the Bonapartes and to the Austrian Imperial Family. Lucjan was effectively placed under a form of 'house arrest' on his enforced return home, however this was unpleasant but lenient treatment by the standards of the time.

[l] She would return to Vienna some years later and died there.

[li] Melanie, Julia and Lucjan received substantial inheritances, according to Jan Kostrowicki. He wrote that "great-grandfather

[Samuel] and great-grandmother were apparently very wealthy people and they had serious capital abroad. After their death, their foreign property was given to their daughters Julia and Melanie, their brother (my grandfather), it seemed inherited the property in Wilenszczyzna[li] ([the estates of] Kowale, Papiernia and Koscieniew)." [li] After his difficulties in Paris and his return to Lithuania he settled at Papiernia, the main family home, where he married (Jozefa Sieklucka), giving up any hopes of moving to Vienna to build a career there. Jan also wrote that his grandfather Lucjan sold Kowale and Papiernia, that is, 2/3 of his property, and donated the sale proceeds to his sisters, Melanie and Julia. After Julia's death, all of this was inherited by Melanie. As Jan wrote, "here again, some mysterious factors had to play a decisive role in my grandfather's actions". It would seem that substantial funds were needed.

As Jan would write to Anatol Stern in 1958, if you compare these circumstances with Melanie's son's birth, and then "with the efforts to get the Vatican to care for him, it seems logical to assume that this money was used to obtain and provide this care". In passing over to his sisters more than half of his inheritance, and so disadvantaging his own wife and children, Lucjan must have felt a significant compulsion.

[lii] Gr.06, Nr. 13 (Kostrowicki); Gr.06, Nr.12A (Elssler) - Friedhof Hietzing

[liii] Rome was then very different to the cosmopolitan city of today, political and legislative capital of a united Italian republic, encapsulating the entire Italian peninsula, teeming with pilgrims, visiting dignitaries, cardinals, archbishops, bishops, abbots, abbesses, priests, monks, nuns and others of the Roman Catholic faithful and thousands upon thousands of

tourists. At the start of the 19th Century Rome stood at the centre of the Papal States, the Pope not just a spiritual leader and Christ's Vicar on Earth, the inheritor of the mantle of St Peter, but also very much a temporal ruler of a large domain.

Napoleon I conquered the Papal States and they were annexed into his Empire, part of France. Declaring his son King of Rome was a calculated slap down to the Pope (and to the dethroned Holy Roman Emperor, permitted to remain as Emperor of a reduced Austria and King of Hungary), directing him to focus on matters of faith, not state. Most of the Papal States were returned to the Pope by the Congress of Vienna. The Vatican had reason to be grateful to Francis and Metternich.

Austria controlled large swathes of Northern Italy and Italian nationalists saw their opportunity to tap into the wider mood of rebellion against foreign totalitarian regimes. In the Papal States liberal views brought demands for independence from the Church, which was resented by many, even the faithful, for exercising too much influence over their lives. In 1848 revolutions broke out on the mainland and in Sicily. King Charles-Albert of Piedmont-Sardinia was the leader, seeking to unite Italy and drive out the Austrians. After losing to the Austrians at the Battle of Custoza in July a truce was signed - Austria remained in control.

A Roman Republic was declared in 1849, of which the famous Giuseppe Garibaldi was a leader. This action failed. Austria and the Papacy shared a common interest in the status quo, although the next two decades would see continued strife and the retreat of the Papal States, with the Pope clinging on to rule in Rome.

For a time, Pius received aid and troops from Napoleon III (ironically), however the commencement of the Franco-Prussian War in July 1870, culminating in the defeat of France and Napoleon's abdication, ended this aid. On 20 September 1870 a three hour long artillery cannonade preceded the Italian Army infiltrating the city, which was occupied the following day. After a plebiscite in which the vast majority of Rome's citizens (over 130,000 voters) voted in favour, Rome was annexed to the newly founded Kingdom of Italy and became Italy's capital on 1 July 1871.

[liv] He lies buried in close proximity to Fanny Elssler and to Samuel Kostrowicki and his family members in the Hietzing Cemetery. His grave reference is Gr. 06, Nr. 15.

[lv] Istanbul, the Ottoman Empire.

[lvi] The name is spelt Kostrowicki (Polish), Кастравіцкі (Russian), Kastravicki, Kostrovitski, Kostrowitzky (phonetically) and other variants.

[lvii] Austrian military intelligence, which oversaw the *Kundschaftsbüro*, tasked with monitoring foreign states.

[lviii] Angelika de Kostrowitzky 1858 - 1919, c. 26 years younger than [Alberto] Kostrowicki.

[lix] The Kostrowicki Family is an old Ruthenian (White Russian) noble (boyar) family with several branches holding different crests. The branch of Angelika Kostrowitzky (sic) came from Kostrowicze near Słonim, south east of Grodno in Belarus and had the crest Prawdzic (descended from Hrybun - Bakunowicz - see *Le Flaneur des Deux Rives*, Bulletin d'Etudes Apollinariennes, No.1 Mars 1954, p.12 - *Les ancêtres*

maternels d'Apollinaire by Maria Kostrowicka-Dabrowa).
The branch of Melanie Kostrowicka (and her son) came from
Koscieniew, near Lida, west of Minsk and used the crest
Bajbuza. The Kostrowicki family is descended from the
Obakunovich Family of Novgorod, boyars (including
posadniks, centurions and the Tribune (hertzog, or dux
bellorum) Oleksander Obakunovich), referred to in The
Chronicle of Novgorod.

Obakunovich means 'son of Obakun' (or Avvakun) 'lover of
God' in old Rus'ian).   In old English the name Godwin
derives from 'Godwine', comprised of two Proto-Germanic
elements: 'gudą' (god, deity, divine being) plus 'winiz'
(friend). Obakunovich is a Rusified version of Godwin. The
name Kostrowicki was derived from their crest of Kostrowiec
(the Cross).

Harold Godwinson, Earl of East Anglia and (briefly) King of
England (1066) and three of his brothers, Tostig, Gyrth and
Leofwine, died in battle (at Stamford Bridge and Senlac Hill /
Hastings) within a few days of each other in 1066. A famous
feud between Harold and Tostig brought about the tragic end
of Anglo-Saxon rule in England. They were sons of Godwin,
Earl of Wessex. Their descendants found refuge in Denmark,
Norway, Rus (Kiev, Novgorod), Lithuania and elsewhere in
Europe.

Gytha of Wessex, daughter of Harold Godwinson, married
Vladimir Monomakh, Prince of Smolensk, in c. 1074/5. The
eldest son of Vladimir Monomakh and Gytha of Wessex,
Mstislav I of Kiev 1076 - 1132), who appeared in Norse sagas
under the name Harald, that of his grandfather, reigned in
Novgorod from 1088 to 1093.

Godwin, Harold's son, having tried, with his brothers Edmund
and Magnus, to avenge their father and recover their

inheritance, came to Rus from Scandinavia.

Members of the Obakunovich Family came to Mstislav Province of Lithuania in the 15th Century. Ivan served as Podskarbi (Silver Treasurer) to Prince Yurij Lukgvenovich Mstislavsky (aka Jurij Semionovich (Lengvenaitis)) (Prince of Novgorod (1432 - 1440) and Duke of Mstislav (1431 - 1442, 1443*, 1445 - 1460)). There were strong links between the Obakunovich/Kostrowicki family, Mstislav and that branch of the Lithuanian Royal House (descended from Giedymin) that was the princely/ducal house of Mstislav and provided princes to Novgorod (forebears of the Mstislavski princes). Wasil Kostrowicki (see also below) was the ancestor of Melanie Kostrowicka, via his son Jan-Rafał.

* See 'Gedimináičiai, Enciklopedinis Žinynas, pubd. Vilnius 2005, ISBN 5-420-01558-7, p.71, where it is stated (in Lithuanian) in this section on Jurgis Lengvenaitis (Prince/Duke Yuri Lengvenovich) that "1443 jam buvo dovanota, atgavo tėvonija Mstislavlio kunigaikštystę. Po konflikto su didžiuoju kunigaikščiu Kazimieru 1445 vėl teko bėgti, bet 1446 kunigaikštystę atgavo." (English: "In 1443 the Duchy of Mstislavl was granted to him and so he regained his father's land. Due to conflict with the Grand Duke Kazimierz he had to flee again in 1445, but he regained the Duchy in 1446."

Kostrowicki is a Polonised name derived from the family's crest, Kostrowiec (the Cross). The Cross appeared on Anglo-Saxon coinage and the crest of the House of Wessex since 838 AD when, at a Council in Kingston (and again later in that year), King Ecgberht of Wessex confirmed to the Church certain lands and privileges in return for its ongoing support for his dynasty. The record of the Council of Kingston, and another charter of that year, include identical language: that a condition of the grant is that "we ourselves and our heirs shall always hereafter have firm and unshakable friendships from Archbishop Ceolnoth and his congregation at Christ Church."

The first known person to use the name Kostrowicki was, appropriately, Protas Kostrowicki. Mstislav Boyarin* Yakov Fedorovich Obakunovich Levtik, accompanied by his son Protas Kostrowicki podstarosta (under-sheriff) of Mstislav and King's Courtier, on 8 March 1561 appeared before King Zygmunt II August (King of Poland and Grand Duke of Lithuania) and received from him a Privilege** confirming Yakov as the holder of the village of Steckovo (alias Kostrowicze) in Mstislav Province, first granted by Kniaz Yurij Lukgvenovich Mstislavsky in 1443 to his Treasurer (Podskarbi) Ivan, Yakov's grandfather, which Privilege was also later confirmed to Ivan by Kniaz Ivan Yurievich Mstislavsky. Protas' brother, Bohdan z Kostrowic Kostrowicki, was the father of Wasil Kostrowicki (married to Regina Zambrzycka), above. Yakov Obakunovich also had a third son, Małofiej. [*A 'Boyarin', or Boyar, was a member of the highest rank of the feudal Kievan, Moscovian and Novgorodian (Ruthenian) aristocracies, second only to the ruling princes from the 10th century to the 17th century.**recorded in the 41st book (pages 217 – 218v) of the Metrika of the Grand Duchy of Lithuania – the original is in The Russian State Historical Archive or RGIA (*Rossiiskii Gosudarstvennyi Istoricheskii Arkhiv)*]

lx Possibly he had been or still was a Colonel in the Papal Guard - perhaps either the Palatine Guard (infantry) or the Noble Guard (cavalry), as distinct from the Swiss Guard.

lxi The estate of Doroszkowice, pow. dziśnieński (Dzisna

County), Lithuania.

[lxii] On 31 August 1880 the Registrar of the City of Rome was 'informed' of the birth, five days earlier, of a male child whose mother wanted to remain anonymous and whose father was 'unknown' (entered as 'N.N.'). The child's name was given as Guillaume-Albert Dulcigni. On 29 September 1880 the same child, now said to have been born on 25 August at 5 a.m., was baptised with the names of Guillelmus Apollinaris Albertus de Kostrowitzky, son of Angelica de Kostrowitzky (sic). The father was still not identified. A month later, on 2 November, Madame de Kostrowitzky officially recognised her son. She would always call him Wilhelm.

[lxiii] Napoleon III (1808–1873), his wife Empress Eugénie (1826–1920) and their son the Prince Imperial (1856–1879) were exiled from France in 1870. They came to live in Chislehurst, in England. Napoleon III died in 1873 and was buried at St Mary's in Chislehurst.

After the tragic death of her son, Napoleon IV, or Prince Imperial, Eugénie built a lasting monument to her family. She founded the Benedictine Abbey of St. Michael in Chislehurst in 1881, there erecting a mausoleum, the Imperial Crypt, for her late husband and son (based upon on the altar of St Louis, where her husband had wished to be interred). Empress Eugénie was later interred together with her husband and son. They lie in granite sarcophagi (arranged by Queen Victoria).

[lxiv] Gr. 6, Nr. 12A.

[lxv] None of whose given names coincided with those of Wilhelm (Apollinaire) or his younger brother Albert.

[lxvi] Was this connected with the fact that Melanie Kostrowicka did not leave her Vienna property (and perhaps any Roman assets) to her nephew Marcin, as had been hoped for by her relatives (per Jan Kostrowicki's letter), but rather to the Church, of which she was a secular Canoness? Had she in fact made an arrangement with the Church to provide for the welfare and education of her grandsons, Wilhelm Albert Apolinary Kostrowicki (Apollinaire) and his younger brother Albert and for their mother? The names Albert(o) and Wilhelm (Guillermo) become strong candidates for those of the son of Franz and Melanie - names that Franz's mother, Marie-Louise, had given to her daughter (Albertina Maria, Countess of Montenuovo, later Countess of Fontanalleto) and to her son (Wilhelm Albert, Prince of Montenuovo) by Adam Albert von Neipperg, Franz's half-sister and half-brother, both born illegitimate and later legitimated. Wilhelm Albert named one of his daughters Albertyna Leopoldyna Wilhelmina (married name Wielopolska). Franz's mother, still mourning the loss of her husband, von Neipperg a couple of years earlier, grandmother to Franz's son, was a necessary ally and guardian for this child. Such families chose and repeated given names for good reasons, to clarify lines within families or to celebrate or remember an ancestor or relative.

[lxvii] There is a notable difference between what was written by Jan Kostrowicki, relating what his late father, Marcin, Melanie's nephew, told him and what Apollinaire wrote. Apollinaire tells us there was a secret wedding "People are saying that in a secret ceremony the Duke of Reichstadt married a daughter of one of our great families, and that a son born of this marriage was brought up unknown even to those in attendance at court."

The position of the son of this union would have been fundamentally different if it was legitimate, the true and legitimate heir to Napoleon I and Napoleon II, the King of Rome, or Duke of Reichstadt, as you will, but in any event the rightful Bonaparte claimant to his grandfather's legacy and also legitimately of Hapsburg descent.

In Poland, so soon after the failed Uprising, it could have contributed to relighting the flames, offered hope, this child of the heir to Napoleon and a daughter of Poland - Lithuania from an old noble family. None of this would have been lost on Emperor Francis or Metternich, or indeed, the Tsar and the King of Prussia. The Vatican would have shared this view.

lxviii Addressed to the surrealist poet and author Anatol Stern and shared by him on pp. 218 - 229 of his book "Dom Apollinaire'a" (House of Apollinaire), published in Krakow in 1973. This is an extract from that longer letter.

lxix Marcin Kostrowicki h. Bajbuza (1855 - 1905).

lxx Prince Nikolai Vasilyevich Repnin (1734 – 1801) was an Imperial Russian statesman and general who played a key role in the dissolution of the Polish-Lithuanian Commonwealth (Rzeczpospolita). In 1763 Empress Catherine (the Great) sent him to Poland as Minister Plenipotentiary, where he was the de facto governor. This privilege or letter was probably dated from that time. The original in the possession of this branch of the Kostrowicki family was lost in WWI and the consequent destruction and upheavals affecting Kosceniew, the family's estate situated near Lida. It was the practice of the Crown Chancellery to keep copies and records of such documents and this original may yet be found to have survived in one such collection still known today, e.g., the Moscow State Archives.

Many of these items have not yet been catalogued or published.

lxxi Count (in Latin) (the nearest British equivalent is an earl).

lxxii A typical look of Polish and Lithuanian magnates and nobility in the 16th Century.

lxxiii Manor house home of that branch of the Kostrowicki family, West of Vilnius.

lxxiv Also visited by your narrator's grandfather, Samuel Andrzej Lew-Ostik-Kostrowicki, his brothers (Daniel and Andrzej) and sisters (Maryla, Barbara and Krystyna).

lxxv In 1812 Count Samuel Kostrowicki was a lieutenant in the Horse Artillery of the Lithuanian Army, formed to fight for the freedom of Lithuania and which became part of the Grande Armee of Napoleon I that marched to Moscow. In January 1813 his unit was folded into the forces of the Grand Duchy of Warsaw, under Marshal Prince Jozef Poniatowski, in which Samuel was appointed a Captain of the Honour Guard of Prince Poniatowski and a Chevalier of the Legion d'Honneur. He would later be granted entry to France, listed as a 'Prussian Count'. A photograph of the undress uniform, epaulette and waistcoat of Lieutenant Samuel Kostrowicki, as an officer of the Horse Artillery Regiment of the Duchy of Warsaw (1810 - 1814) may be seen on p. 179 of 'Napoleon i Polacy' (Napoleon and the Poles) by Dom Wydawniczy Bellona, Warsaw and the Muzeum Wojska Polskiego w Warszawie (Polish Army Museum), ISBN 83-11-10121-3.

lxxvi Volynskaya region, which is situated in the north-west of Ukraine, borders on Poland and Belarus. Since the earliest times the region was a part of Kievan Rus. Later it was included into the Galitsko-Volynskoe principality ruled by the Rurikovich dynasty, then it became a part of Lithuania, Poland, and subsequently the Russian Empire.

[lxxvii] Believed to be St. Cyr.

[lxxviii] Melanie Kostrowicka (1813 - 1889) turned 18 in 1831; she was three years younger than Fanny Elssler.

[lxxix] The only such person at the Austrian Court was Franz, Duke of Reichstadt.

[lxxx] Marcin Kostrowicki, the father of Jan, the author of this letter, died in 1905, the year after the conversation to which Jan refers took place. His widow, Princess Maria Massalska (1863 - 1915) survived him by 10 years. His sons Stanisław (1888 - 1918) and Jan (1889 - 1967) were 17 and 16 and their sister, Zofia (1886 - 1943) 15 when their father died. The opportunity for Marcin to reveal more was lost with him. Only Jan survived WWI and WWII and into the years of the Soviet Union and Communism to disclose what he wrote carefully, for posterity. Jan was the father of two sons, Prof. Jerzy Samuel Kostrowicki (1918 - 2002), geographer, and Prof. Andrzej Samuel Kostrowicki (1921 - 2007), biogeographer. Jerzy (married to Irena Halina Czapska) had one daughter, Ania Kostrowicka.

[lxxxi] pp. 224 - 226, 'Dom Apollinaire'a', by Anatol Stern.

[lxxxii] c. 100 km south of Vilnius. When the Sieklucki family returned to Strzelica ('The Shooter'), theirs for c. 300 years, they found the remains of buildings and ruins - valuables, family portraits, old documents, and the library were destroyed. Outside the manor house, a dozen farm buildings were also destroyed. The Germans had only weak control of

the area and lawlessness was rife, with gangs of armed stragglers and bandits operating.

[lxxxiii] In the Nowogródek (Navahrudak) region, in North-Eastern Belarus.

[lxxxiv] Zofia Jundziłowna h. Łabędź was the wife of Jan Hrehorowicz Ościk (in Lithuanian, Jonas Astikas) (d.1611), whose son by him (Jerzy Janowicz Ościk – see pp. 310 & 439, 'Herbarz Rycerstwa W.X. Litewskiego' by Wojciech Wijuk Kojałowicz (published in Krakow in 1897)) assumed the name Kostrowicki (the progenitor of the Lew-Ostik Kostrowicki line). Zofia married again (her third husband) after Jan's death.

[lxxxv] The Sieklucki family.

Also by Jeremy Moczarski:

A Man of Power and a Goblin on a Fork

Poetry in the blood

Spring blossoms, Summer fruits

Printed in Great Britain
by Amazon